Rising Through Adversity

How do we journey with hope, through the
difficulties of life, to find true riches?

Judith Beecham

malcolm down
PUBLISHING

First published 2021 by Malcolm Down Publishing Ltd.
www.malcolmdown.co.uk

24 23 22 21   7 6 5 4 3 2 1

British Library Cataloguing in Publication Data
A catalogue record for this book is available from the British Library.

ISBN 978-1-912863-97-6

Cover design by Esther Kotecha
Art direction by Sarah Grace

Printed in the UK

To those who are struggling, or searching for more

Endorsements

I love this book! For me, it resonates with so much I personally hold dear. I love that it is grounded in both Scripture and in experience, and that it provides so many moments for reflection and application. I believe, for many, it will provide language and a fresh framework for interpreting life experiences in the light of God's love and goodness.

More than anything else God is after our hearts, and this book gently assists us in navigating that divine process of inner freedom and fruitfulness. I believe Judith has put together, not just a book for reading, but a highly practical guidebook of real nuggets, to assist the reader in the sacred journeying of the heart. I recommend it highly. It's a book to come back to many times over.

Wes Boxall, Senior Pastor Golden Valley Church, Life Coach/Mentor

I found this book to be a sensitive invitation to journey alongside the author as she shared her personal experience of pain and suffering and, whilst at the same time, having the author journey with me as I navigate through the complexity of faith. The watering holes of the 'Pause and encounter' sessions, the reflective pictures and the wisdom and insight portrayed gave hope that an encounter with God is possible, wherever we are on our spiritual walk. I would recommend it to anyone who is struggling with their faith in whatever way, and who are sensing a need to draw closer to God. The book is an easy yet profound walk with someone who has understanding and sensitivity in an area of faith that is so often neglected.

Margaret Wade, spiritual director

Rising Through Adversity is a beautifully written, inspirational book. The author invites us to journey with her, finding the presence of God as she shares wisdom gleaned from her own life experiences. Her gentle writing, encouragement, vulnerability, along with the artwork and Pause and encounter sections, all serve to facilitate a space for God to work in the life of the reader. Insightful and powerful, this book is like a signpost for those seeking a genuine encounter with God.

Sheila Jacobs, award-winning writer, editor, and author of
A Little Book of Rest

Struggles are part of life, but sometimes they seem to come in job lots and threaten to overwhelm us. Navigating the way forward and staying connected to the love and purposes of God in those moments can be particularly challenging. Rich in truth and compassionate in tone, this book will help you discover the treasure that Isaiah says can only be found in darkness. Judith's authentic insights and honest wisdom will not only bring purpose to your struggle but also practical tools to strengthen you through it. I believe this book will encourage you!

Hils Grew, church leader, speaker, author of Known

Contents

Introduction

This book has been birthed out of adversity, including a very long illness, which has been tough in many, many ways. It has not only been a difficult illness to live through, but it has raised many questions. Why? Where are You, God, in this? Why is my healing so slow? How can I walk free of this relentless battering? What is really going on? What is going on from God's viewpoint? What is God saying? Does He care?

Challenges in our lives can bring us to forks in the road. We can easily go down routes where our hearts gradually, or maybe dramatically, harden off towards God. Maybe we are going through the motions of living life with God, but distance and resentment are growing in our hearts, or perhaps anger is setting in. Or perhaps we haven't yet found God and are longing for Him to be there for us, but the fog of our circumstances is causing blocks towards God.

Alternatively, we may be trying to keep a positive outlook, to keep going in whatever way we can, but maybe not being honest with ourselves and real before God. We can be pushing down pain, supressing it, ignoring it, and just trying to move on. Either way, we are not finding real hope, we are just about coping and trying to move forward; but with chains or dark clouds impeding us.

As we struggle to find a path through our challenges, a light can draw us to a route where we find God in the very midst of it all; of finding gold revealed in the ashes; finding wounds transformed to strengths; and finding that Jesus truly came to 'set the oppressed free'[1] and provide a way to rise up through it all.

One purpose of this book is to bring hope, especially to those having a hard time. My heart is very much with you and I have an expectation for good things for you. I have found that this journey has led to depths and riches I did not expect.

The chapters are succinct and allow space for reflection. My pictures are scattered throughout to hopefully touch the heart and speak what is more easily said through art than in words. Whilst there is a journey of the understanding, there is also a journey of the heart that I would love to take you on.

This book is also about thriving, about finding more of the potential for our life; it is not just for those who are struggling. We don't need to go through deep suffering for the topics in this book to be relevant. In many ways this book is about not getting stuck or settling, but finding the 'far more' that God has for us.

Although suffering is a very difficult and perplexing subject, it is an important one to reflect on. Our perspective on suffering affects our view of life and can challenge our view of God. Our subconscious assumption can be that God should always be nice and the goal in life is just to be happy. Maybe we see suffering as God's will, or believe God should prevent all of it. Or perhaps we find it a very difficult area that has coloured our view of God. So this subject is a pivotal one. It is a tragedy when people have

---

1. Luke 4:18.

turned away from God because of their conclusions or hurt in this area. Let's look deeper into this issue.

I have scattered my own story throughout this book, especially those moments that may bring more understanding of suffering and walking through adversity. But I have not written extensively about my story. I want it to be about your story. I am very aware at my weakest times of just not being able to cope with other people's pain. I struggled to read and take anything in, and I simply did not have the emotional resilience to cope with more heartache. However, anything bringing real hope, bringing light into my situation, anything that would help me find more of God's love, comfort, truth and healing was like water in the desert, lifelines to hold on to. It is these lifelines and signposts that this book is about.

My journey has wound its way through a very long illness of Lyme disease and chronic fatigue syndrome (ME) with many years of not remotely feeling myself, with every area of strength knocked out of me and continually feeling ill. Sadly, during this time, I also walked alongside my closest friend as she lost her life to cancer, leaving a big hole in my life. In the earlier stage of the illness, deep turmoil, stress and pain from the ending of a relationship was another struggle that profoundly impacted me.

Much of this book has come from walking through these experiences. I have also drawn on the nuggets I have found from drawing alongside many others in all levels of sufferings or woundedness, through facilitating inner healing prayer sessions.

Throughout this book there are *Pause and encounter* moments. It may well be as you read this book and meditate on the pictures that aspects resonate with your own life. These *Pause and encounter* moments are to allow space for God to speak, and for thoughts to land. They are also for practical steps on how to pray. The prayers may seem simple and may be in contrast to hours of processing with other approaches. However, when God speaks to us and acts, it can be incredibly powerful. His truth and power can simply set us free. It is so easy to gather endless head knowledge, but not take the steps for knowledge to become insight, revelation and change. So I would very much encourage you to participate in the *Pause and encounter* activities. They are a starting point, which may reveal a need for further help. Having individual inner healing prayer ministry can take you a lot further. Some places to go for this are listed in Appendix 2.

May light break through as you read this book and, as you pause, may you find truths to hold on to in the arms of an immensely loving God. May you find the inestimable value and riches that can come out of the challenges of life and out of our darkest times . . . that can transform us for good.

The promise of hope.

How the Book Began

After having a complete stranger who didn't know my story say I needed to write a book, and then receiving the same words from two other people, I felt I had to take note. The trouble was, this was ringing slightly true and I was very uncomfortable with it. One issue was that writing was not my favourite pastime, to say the least (and I have to admit I have had much help with editing this book!). The deeper issue was the subject matter. I knew if this was a true commission, it was to be about suffering – an uncomfortable and difficult subject, one we want to avoid. I tread very carefully with this subject as I am well aware that there are extremes of suffering I have no experience of and that this is an incredibly delicate area, carrying immense pain for many.

So with a very reluctant heart, one Tuesday one summer I said to God, 'OK, if this really is from You, I will go on a four-day retreat this weekend and start the book. This is Your one chance!' I would only try booking with two retreat centres that weren't too far away. I knew they would be fully booked and I wouldn't get in and I wouldn't have to write the book . . . phew . . . unless I really was meant to write it and God would take me at my word and make a way for it to happen. I phoned the first place and they were, as expected, fully booked for the next three months, a big relief! I phoned the other centre and there was a pause, my heart started to sink, they sounded a little surprised and said they were normally fully booked a long way ahead, but unusually, just half an hour before, they had had a cancellation for the exact four days I'd chosen.

I duly arrived at my room at the retreat centre, walked in and was overwhelmed by the presence of God. That intense, electric, tingling atmosphere, when you know you are on holy ground. His strong presence continued for nearly an hour. The confirmation was complete, I had to write the book. The next four days were a flow, a download of thoughts and coming together of all the streams of thoughts and truths and experiences that had carried me through the tough years. I came to the end of the four days and it then dawned on me that my paintings over the last two months illustrated every theme in the book . . . completely unplanned. I had recently been on a 'prophetic art' retreat where we were encouraged to find God leading in what to paint. This has then led to a download of paintings ever since.

Unexpectedly . . . the book had been born!

Part 1

The Unexpected Journey

Has life's journey taken an unexpected turn? Is the pathway steeper or rockier than expected? Has it passed through some dark valleys or thick mists? Or does it just feel dry, and hard work?

Maybe life's journey has taken you through the 'wilderness', or through the 'fire', or into 'prison'. Maybe your heart is struggling. Perhaps God feels distant, or your faith has been shaken.

Through my own long walk through illness, I have been repeatedly drawn to the biblical story of the Israelites going through the wilderness to the Promised Land. I have been very taken with the symbolic meanings of this journey. They have provided another perspective to what is going on. I have also been pursuing the question of, 'What is the (metaphorical) "Promised Land"?'

Through my stumbles along this journey, I have found there is a way through, a way through to a 'Promised Land'; a way through where we are not destroyed, hardened or grow cold, but we are transformed; a way through that brings deep healing, greater freedom and a new release of the Holy Spirit in and overflowing from our life. There is a powerful transformation available, perhaps more easily accessible than on an easier route. There may be many trips and stumbles along the way, we may feel like we are failing at every turn, but much grace, much love is found as we journey. There is a way through, with God.

So how do we travel well and find the riches of the journey? How do we find that Promised Land that awaits us? What is the Promised Land?

We may think that if we know the 'why', we can cope with the 'how'. We may never be able to understand the 'whys' in this life, or only have very limited glimpses of the bigger picture. We may have to live with the hidden mysteries until we are able to see more from God's perspective. While we may not be able to understand the 'whys', it can greatly help if we can see a little more of how God is bringing good out of everything we go through. If we can know more of how to find God and His riches in the midst of it all, our journey can be transformed, as well as ourselves.

The great people of the Bible experienced unexpected journeys. Moses grew up in the palace with Pharaoh: a life of royalty and riches. He had been adopted. However, he became aware of the suffering of his own people, the Israelites. His people were in slavery to the Egyptians, under a very oppressive rule. His life in the palace then had an unexpected turn. He saw an Egyptian afflicting a fellow Israelite and, in an outburst of anger, he killed the Egyptian. He then had to flee for his life to the desert of Midian where he spent the next forty years tending sheep. Not his own sheep or even his father's sheep, but the sheep of his father-in-law, a disgrace in a patriarchal world. Even worse, shepherds were the lowest of the low in Egypt.[2] A real comedown for a prince.

The shepherd boy, David, was told by the prophet Samuel he would be king of Israel. Things started well. He progressed from looking after his sheep to living in the palace playing the lyre to soothe King Saul's moods. He learnt about palace life and grew in friendship with the king's son, Jonathan. Then he too had to flee for his life and spend time living in caves in the desert and even in the land of Israel's enemies, the Philistines.[3] A band of motley, discontented men gathered around him; how different from court life and the prophecies over his life, that he would be the king of Israel.

Exotic, resilient flowers grow in the desert.

2. Genesis 46:34.
3. 1 Samuel 22-27.

Joseph had two prophetic dreams: one of sheaves of corn bowing down to him; the other of the sun, moon and stars bowing down to him. Then he found himself thrown in a pit by his jealous brothers, taken into slavery in another country, and then wrongly accused and thrown into prison.[4]

Many others in the Bible, to different extents, had unexpected journeys or times in a 'wilderness'. Even Jesus Himself had His forty days in the wilderness, where He encountered evil and the temptations of the devil.[5]

What went on in Moses during those forty years of looking after sheep? What went on in David as he lived in those caves and pondered the words of Samuel over his life? What went on in Joseph, falsely accused and in prison far from home in a foreign land? Happily, their stories didn't end there. You can almost feel the hosts of heaven encouraging them to hang on in, to not lose hope, to not harden their hearts to God; encouraging them to be patient and to let the journey work its transformation in them; encouraging them to yield to what God wanted to do in them through that time. God was preparing them for what lay ahead, refining them and transforming them.

What of God's heart towards them during that time? A heart of an extremely loving father training His children for something truly great, but seeing so much coming against them; and immensely pained at the refining they had to go through to get there? A father so saddened when His children have lost sight of what He has promised, or lost sight and awareness of His love and faithfulness?

4. Genesis 37,39.
5. Matthew 4:1-8.

Surely these people with their unexpected journeys had times when they felt forgotten and abandoned. What were those prophecies about? Where was God's faithfulness? Did God really care?

What became of these same people? Moses led the Israelites out of years of slavery and freed them from the rule of the Egyptians; the same Moses who is referred to as the man who God spoke to face to face.[6] David became the greatest king of Israel and was recorded as a man after God's own heart.[7] Joseph became prime minister of Egypt and saved a vast number of lives, saving the whole region from seven years of famine.

Were these journeys times of abandonment by God, of being forgotten . . .? Very, very far from it. We may not have callings on our lives on such a scale, or journeys as extreme as these. Yet we all have our routes of transformation to walk into our callings, to be changed into the person we were designed to be. More than anything, we have a pathway to lead us into a relationship of intimacy with God and discover the deepest love that heals our souls.

---

6. Exodus 33:11.
7. 1 Samuel 13:14; Acts 13:22.

The snail thinks that he is trapped in a crate, not able to see the way ahead and going nowhere fast.

He is thinking that life is passing him by. He does not realise that he is actually in a truck, taking him to a completely new place.

We don't see the bigger picture.

The Wilderness

Let's follow the biblical journey of the Israelite slaves as God set them free from slavery in Egypt and took them on a journey to the Promised Land. What route did the journey to the Promised Land take?

There was the joyous escape from Egypt, but then they found themselves traversing a desert. Moses, David and Joseph all had their own desert, wilderness or prison experiences. So what are the characteristics of times in the wilderness or prison?

They can be times in life when some things are stripped away or we don't have the freedom to do everything we used to do. It can feel like walking through a night-time experience where, for a period of time, things we rely on to give us a boost, to lift our spirits, to feel fulfilled, are not there as before. Why?

We may find we aren't able to rely as much on other people, or activities, busyness, recognition, status, image, success . . . or whatever we usually rely on to feel good. We find these cannot be the things we depend on for comfort, for joy, for fulfilment. Instead, we must dig deeper.

We are drawn into finding a new place of contentment and being sustained by God in a more profound way. This 'night-time' does not last forever. A new dawn will come. Pressures may lift, or things stripped away may be restored in a different way, or the grief recedes . . . but our sources of strength, our sources of joy and our sources of identity have changed.

We come out of this night with treasures. We are strengthened, having a richer and deeper relationship with God.

The wilderness can be a challenging place, but we can also discover there a sanctuary, holy ground, a place of a deeper inner rest and a place to encounter God.

As the Israelites travelled through the desert to the Promised Land, the intensity of God's presence guiding them was like no other period in their history. God provided a cloud by day to guide them and a pillar of fire by night.[8] They had the Ark of the Covenant actually carried along with them. The Ark was where God presenced Himself among them. The Ark wasn't in a distant place in the temple in Jerusalem, but present in their midst, day by day. The wilderness experience can be a time when God is especially close, even as if we are being carried.

The wilderness was a time of profound change. The Israelites had spent years being slaves, for some of them it was their entire lives. It was a time for losing their slave identity. Changing identity does not happen overnight. Legally they were set free from their slave identity in a day, but learning to live free, to

---

8. Exodus 13:21.

fully embrace their new identity in how they thought and felt, and how they lived it out, took far, far longer. It was a coming out from under oppression, fear, hopelessness, powerlessness, control and the restraints of slavery.

It was a time of learning to make right choices from a place of freedom; choices to walk in responsibility, integrity and obedience to God's ways. It was a time to leave behind a slave's mindset, to embrace one of hope, growth and expectancy. With the daily structure of slavery removed, it was a time of learning to trust and follow a faithful God.It was a journey of promise, with a new homeland as their destination.

However, the heat of the desert, the challenging environment, the same food day after day revealed their hearts. Many attitudes came to the surface that needed to die in the desert. The journey was not easy, and because of their stubbornness and unbelief, it took far longer than it needed. Again and again they learnt the hard way, especially when they proceeded in their own wisdom. It required a deep surrender to God, to go His way in everything. This was the only way for them to get through, not only to survive the desert, but to journey well through the adversity.

*Jesus in the boat with us, as we journey through the night,
to a new dawn and a new land.*

The heat of the desert, like a fire, reveals our hearts; the deeply buried, the unknown, the untested, the fears, the insecurities . . . We fear the fire, we want to run from it, until we see, in the very heart of it, the passion of love, a love so strong, so tender, more adoring than we had ever, ever imagined. A fire to bring us home, to dislodge the lies at the core of our being, to release us from the chains that hold us down, to bring healing to inner pain, brokenness and fear . . . A fire to make us whole. Such a fire of God's love calls us, walks with us and draws us into freedom.

So often, it's not until we are feeling the fire that we look within, that we dig deep, that we cry out to God to cleanse us and change us and heal us. There we find the Father standing with His oil of healing, waiting for us with open arms.

Our Father God has been longing to heal us of the wounds of slavery. He has been longing to free us from the chains that have held us down, the chains of anxiety, of low self-worth, of rejection, of rage, of a critical or judgemental mindset, of jealousy, of self-pity, of lust . . . our Achilles' heels.

He aches to release us from the powers that have ruled over us and that we ourselves have not been able to break free from. He so desires to bring truth into our deepest thoughts, into our core beliefs; to expose those false beliefs that have crept into our thinking when we have interpreted our experiences wrongly.

We may have concluded deep down that we are not of great value, that we are insignificant and God doesn't really care. Such underlying, even subconscious, wrong beliefs are incredibly damaging and God so wants to heal us and set us free from them.

God was looking for people He could trust to handle the abundance and responsibilities of the Promised Land. A people who would handle the riches well, who He could trust to rule it. A people healed of their slavery, in all its forms.

Being transformed in the confines of the chrysalis into a beautiful butterfly.

Pause and encounter

For each of these 'Pause and encounter' moments it is good to have some time set aside for quiet. Ask God to help you to hear Him and to silence other 'voices'. Welcome the Holy Spirit to be with you more.

There are some suggested questions and prayers to take to God, but these are not prescriptive or a formula; they just may be helpful pointers to follow, but go with the flow of what is real. Address the questions to whoever you find it easiest to relate to — God, heavenly Father, Jesus or Holy Spirit — I have said Jesus, but choose who you feel most at home with. For some the concept of God being like an immensely loving father can be very difficult, until healing of their own father wounds takes place. It may be easier initially to relate to the nurturing, comforting presence of the Holy Spirit, the Spirit of God.

It is important not to answer the questions yourself or analyse or self-diagnose, but very purposely ask the questions to God, then just wait and see what first drops into your mind without trying. It might be words, a picture, a memory, or sense or an emotion. Don't worry if you don't receive anything straightaway or if you know it's just your own thoughts. The process to unblock our 'hearing' can come with time. If it stays a struggle, having some inner healing prayer ministry can be extremely helpful — see Appendix 2.

Ask Jesus:

Am I in a chrysalis where I am being transformed?

Provision – the Manna

Whilst the journey through the wilderness was more than challenging, it was also a time of miraculous provision of the Israelites' needs. It was a season where they could not provide for themselves; where they were taken beyond their self-sufficiency. Their own abilities would not get them through and out of the wilderness. There was no way they could survive in their own strength.

There is something uniquely special about those times when we are weak, when it is completely beyond us to meet our needs ourselves, when we are vulnerable, when we cannot sort out life, when we cannot cope on our own. These are times when we so often see God step in and do the amazing 'coincidences' of provision and even the miraculous – when He provides what we are unable to provide for ourselves.

Trust grows from seeing ongoing evidence of God's continual faithfulness. The Israelites would have seen this, that day after day after day, God provided 'manna' for them to eat. He miraculously provided water when there was no drinkable water in sight. A flock of quails came when they were longing to eat meat.[9] God always provided for their needs.

---

9. Exodus 16; 15:25.

Because of your great compassion you did not abandon them in the wilderness. By day the pillar of cloud did not fail to guide them on their path, nor the pillar of fire by night to shine on the way they were to take. You gave your good Spirit to instruct them. You did not withhold your manna from their mouths, and you gave them water for their thirst. For forty years you sustained them in the wilderness; they lacked nothing, their clothes did not wear out nor did their feet become swollen.

Nehemiah 9:19-21

Learning to Lean

Our props have been taken away, maybe the smokescreen of busyness, or the accomplishments or the roles or status removed; we've lost our false sources of identity and the 'fixes' that give us a boost. We see ourselves as we truly are. The grot in us comes to the surface. Self-sufficiency fails.

Yet here the Father stands with open arms. He has been waiting and waiting for us to know that we are nothing without Him; waiting for us to come to Him in our brokenness, in our weakness, and be held in His embrace. He is waiting for us to reach that place where He can begin the deep healing work we all need; waiting to lead us into a new way of being, where we lean on Him. He is waiting for us to learn to be led by Him. The Israelites were given a pillar of cloud by day and a pillar of fire by night to guide them.[10] We learn to hear His voice in a new way. We learn we need to be led by His Spirit, because our own wisdom is not enough.

Our strength and wisdom, our resources, our existing ways of doing life are simply not adequate to thrive in the desert. We may find we need a closer walk with God, a greater level of being led by Him and being guided and carried through this wilderness

---

10. Exodus 13:21.

time. It is a time of growing to trust God more deeply, that He really does have the way through this. We are being drawn to find Him in a deeper way in the midst of it all.

Learning to lean is finding a more profound way of doing life with Jesus. In the details of our life, we are looking to Him, listening to Him, relying on Him, obeying Him, loving Him, and following the promptings of His Holy Spirit.

We are yielding to His love.

Learning to lean on Jesus.

Who is this coming up from the wilderness
like a column of smoke,
perfumed with myrrh and incense
made from all the spices of the merchant?

Song of Songs 3:6

Who is this coming up from the desert
leaning on her beloved?

Song of Songs 8:5

Pause and encounter

It is important not to treat these prayers as a formula, but to pray from the heart. Try to have a wide open heart to God, with an attitude of 'show me my blind spots, show me what I'm missing'.

Ask Jesus:

Is there any area of my life where I need to lean on You more?

If an area comes to mind, try to make a decision from the heart to want to do that area of life with Jesus and with His help and guidance.

Jesus, I am sorry for trying to handle . . . (e.g. my finances, my relationship, my health, my work, my family) in my own strength. I ask You to come into the centre of this situation and I choose to take hold of Your hand and walk through this together with You. I choose to lean on You and I ask for Your daily help and wisdom and guidance and power.

Is there any area of my life I need to yield to You and ask You to be Lord over?

I am sorry for any way I have wanted to be in control in this area and so now I ask You to be Lord over this area of my life. I choose to submit to Your will and Your best for me.

Digging Deeper

Viktor Frankl, a Jewish psychologist and holocaust survivor, observed in his book *Man's Search for Meaning*[11] how people coped with their concentration camp experience. Of the people who did not dig deeper, he said they preferred to live in the past, disconnecting from now. They found no meaning in life in the present. They failed to see that especially challenging circumstances often give a person the opening to spiritually develop and progress.

Our challenges, or the pain and struggles in our loved ones, are often triggers that drive us to a deeper place of prayer, of searching, of seeking God, of coming into a deeper relationship with Him.

In order to produce diamonds, the raw material of rough black graphite has to be buried deep under mountains, where the temperature is hotter and the pressure is greater. The graphite transforms into a new internal structure of its atoms. Impurities will be flushed out and it is simply recreated to have a new nature. Grapes are pressed to produce wine and olives to produce oil. The pressing produces substances of far greater value.

---

11. Viktor Frankl, *Man's Search for Meaning* (London: Rider, 2004), *p. 80.*

The pressing reveals the inadequacy of our self-sufficiency. As this dependency on ourselves proves insufficient, it leaves space that can allow a new level of filling with the Holy Spirit, more of the Spirit of God within us.

As we dig deeper, our eyes are opened to ourselves.

Moses, David and Joseph were greatly pressed during their wilderness and prison experiences and clearly dug deep with God. They came to a deep place of relationship with God, a place of anointing. Moses came out of his many years in Midian looking after sheep saying to God: 'I can't speak to Pharaoh . . . I can't do what you are calling me to.'[12] His pride in his abilities and self-sufficiency had gone. He walked forward into his calling, utterly dependent on God.

As we dig deeper, we are invited into a new level of experience with God.

In the earlier stage of the illness, I went to a church meeting where there was a visiting speaker who had a significant prophetic gifting. At the end of the meeting many people went forward for prayer. When she came to pray for me, I didn't say anything about my situation, and she waited to hear from God. She then looked deeply compassionate and said something along the lines of it being huge, what I was going through, and that Father God wanted me to know His immense love for me. She gave me the longest hug and just held me and held me . . . and the tears flowed. God was pouring His strength and love and compassion into me at a deep level. He was saying, 'I know . . . I really know . . . and I deeply, deeply care . . . And you can do this; I am absolutely and unquestionably with you.' I could see in my

12. Exodus 4:13.

mind's eye a map of the Sinai desert and I knew then this wasn't going to be a quick fix, or an instant healing, but a significant journey. I knew He could have relieved me of it, but for reasons He wasn't saying, I needed to walk through it, because it was profoundly important and of eternal value. I was going to have to dig deep with God.

God's love and sustaining power for us through the valley.

Choices

So, how do we navigate this desert? How do we travel well?

Maybe, fundamentally, by recognising that this life is not about the pursuit of happiness, or achievement or whatever else we may be pursuing; recognising that it is not necessarily meant to be easy. A far greater purpose for this life is to be transformed to become more like Jesus. A life of true worth comes from preferring His way to our own way. Pursuing and being pursued by the love of God, we then experience more of His love and joy, which is not dependent on circumstances.

Navigating this desert well involves making many healthy choices. So, what of the choices? These choices matter; they really matter. It's the difference between finding joy, despite it all, and being weighed down. It's the difference between being transformed by the journey, and being destroyed by it. It's the difference between our heart shutting down in despair, and it opening up to an invitation to find greater wholeness. Here are some of the choices, not lightly said, not always easy, but crucial:

- We can choose to moan and complain, or hold on by faith.

- We can focus on the door that is shut, or move our focus to where God wants it to be, where God is at work.

- We can focus on desert hardships, or on the direction the journey is taking us.

- We can rail against the prison walls, or treasure the prison cell for the sanctuary and time with God that it provides.

- We can focus on the waves and sink, or fix our eyes on Jesus and walk on the water.[13]

- We can look back at the time of 'slavery in Egypt' and think it would be better to be there than en route to the Promised Land.[14]

- We can compare our lives with those of others, or be grateful for what God has given us.

- We can hold on to resentment and bitterness, or let these go and choose instead to trust in God's goodness.

- We can want to understand and know why we are where we are, or we can trust that God knows the bigger picture and is lovingly taking us to the best He has for us.

- We can feed on anxiety, or we can pray.

- We can focus on what we can't do, or what we can do.

- We can focus on what we haven't got, or what we have got.

- We can grip tightly onto what He is taking away, or let it go and look to what He is giving instead.

- We can have no hope, or look to the God of hope and hold on to what He has promised.

Very often, even most of the time, God is speaking words of encouragement and comfort to us to carry us through the

13.   Matthew 14:29-30.
14.   Numbers 11:18.

wilderness and along our journey. But sometimes, as when Jesus walked across the lake to the disciples in the boat during the storm, He speaks a challenge: 'Where is your faith?'[15] Sometimes we need the challenge. It's our responsibility to guard our thoughts. Our thoughts are like the rudder on a boat, they are critical. They will lead us into the pit, or to a place of peace and trust and hope.

Joseph, when in prison, could have railed against the prison, against the injustice of his situation, punching, kicking, raging at the walls . . . and bruising himself. Being emotionally honest with ourselves and before God is vital and healthy, but being stuck there is not. Making escape from prison the top priority and goal for each day is natural, but God leads us beyond that.

He leads us to live for *His* goals and *His* best for each day. For Joseph, that might have been to spend deeper time with God, learning to hear His voice more, and growing in the gift of interpreting dreams. It might have been to pray for and to show kindness to his fellow prisoners. It might have been praying for his family and choosing to forgive his brothers for throwing him into the pit to die. It might have been asking God to show him his own blind spots and things in his own character that God wanted to work on. It would also have included growing in depth of prayer for his release.

God was training him for his next role as prime minister at a time of national crisis; not that Joseph would have had any idea whatsoever about that. Yet that was the actual reality of the situation.

We have real choices in *how* we live through time in the wilderness.

---

15.   Luke 8:22-25.

*Like Elijah during the drought,
praying for rain and expectant for the rain cloud.*[16]

---

16. 1 Kings 18:41-44.

Pause and encounter

Ask Jesus:

Where am I focusing on a shut door?

What different choices do I need to make in my thought life?

I'm sorry for focusing on . . . and letting my thoughts run down the negative tracks of . . .

What do you want me to focus on instead?

I choose to focus on . . . (e.g. Your love and promises and that You will provide for my needs)

Is there a negative filter I'm viewing my life or You through?

Is there a false belief that is at the root of it?

I reject the false belief that . . .

Is there anyone I need to forgive in relation to this belief?

I choose to forgive . . . for . . . and for how it has affected me.

What is the truth?

I receive the truth that . . .

I hand the negative filter of . . . to You, Jesus, and I choose not to view life through it. I choose not to let my thoughts run down those tracks any longer. Please help me and remind me when I do.

Holding on to Truth

Jesus, when speaking about Himself as a good shepherd, said 'his sheep follow him because they know his voice'.[17] This is a time to cry out to God and say, 'I need to know Your voice more; I need to hear You more clearly.' His words of encouragement, His words of love, His promises and the hope He imparts to us, these are what get us through each day.

Maybe we don't recognise His voice, or negative thoughts have drowned Him out. Maybe, like Elijah,[18] we are looking for the loud voice in the 'earthquake' and in the 'fire', but have not made space to draw aside and listen for the 'gentle whisper'. Let's *ask* to hear His voice more. James wrote, 'You do not have because you do not ask God.'[19] Then let's be ready for Jesus to show us how He is speaking to us.

At the moment Jesus died, the veil in the temple in front of the Holy of Holies was torn in two.[20] This symbolised the way opening up for all to be able to come into the presence of God. It was no longer just for the priests. So we can all become like priests in God's eyes; forgiven and cleansed, and with the way

---

17. John 10:4.
18. I Kings 19:11-12.
19. James 4:2.
20. Mark 15:38.

open for us, through Jesus, to come into the presence of God and hear His voice. He is waiting with open arms for us to do so.

If we are struggling to come into the presence of God and hear His voice, we may need to spend time checking our heart for wrong attitudes, resentments and/or unforgiveness and lay all of that at Jesus' feet and ask for forgiveness. As with a kettle, we don't throw it away if it hasn't come to the boil in the first ten seconds.

We may need to persevere. We get closer until it's natural to know His voice.

From a place of sincerely wanting to know truth, let's ask what He wants to say to us. Then we listen for that 'gentle whisper' which can come in so many ways and maybe not straight away. It may be a verse from the Bible, that seems like it is highlighted on the page, that is so relevant to the situation. It might be a thought or visual impression that drops straight into our mind when we are praying, that speaks to our heart. It might be something else we read that feels like it was written for us. It might even be something in the metaphors of nature that have parallels with our experience: seeing the gardening process, or observing the changes in the seasons. A key way to discern His voice is when we sense peace, when there is no 'check' in our spirit or unease, but a sense of assurance that we have heard.

The Bible says in the voice of two or three witnesses a thing is established.[21] If God is saying something to us, He will confirm it and speak it in different ways. So it is important to look for confirmation and not assume everything we think we hear from God is from Him. Asking for the gift of hearing as well as the gift

---

21.   2 Corinthians 13:1.

of discernment is key. Then we look out for those confirmations to know if we really are hearing from God. We practise, we make mistakes, but we learn along the way.

However, there can be things that are blocking us from hearing His voice. Wrong attitudes or actions can cause a block. Anger towards God can easily get in the way of hearing and there are a variety of other types of blocks which are highlighted through these pages.

Working through the *Pause and encounter* exercises and using the prayers in Appendix 1 can help unblock our hearing. We also all hear in different ways, so what might be easy for one person and suit their brain and personality, may not be how God speaks to someone else.

It may also be very helpful to have other people who do hear easily to pray with us to help get to the root of any blocks. An inner healing prayer session[22] can be very helpful for this. So let's keep asking to be able to hear His voice more clearly and for the gift of discernment to know what is truly from God.

Many people have made mistakes in this area of hearing from God, so we do need to be careful and wise. We absolutely should not make any rash decisions based on 'guidance' from what may have just been our own thoughts. There is need for care in interpreting what we see or hear, not just assuming the interpretation, but asking God for what it means. The voice of the deceiver, the accuser, the devil can also speak. However true 'knowing His voice' is wonderful and as Jesus said 'you will know the truth, and the truth will set you free'.[23]

---

22. See Appendix 2.
23. John 8:32.

In my late teens I remember reading the verse saying that His sheep 'know his voice'[24] and I thought, 'But no, I don't.' So I simply asked Jesus that I would be able to hear His voice. Over the next few days, weeks and years, the answer to this prayer has steadily evolved.

This is not an area to get hung up on or condemned by. In many ways, as we walk with God, our minds are being renewed by God[25] and our thinking becomes more in line with His ways. We walk forward knowing that 'check' in our spirit when things aren't right, and a peace when we are in line with God's will.

Sheep following the Good Shepherd,
with ears pricked to hear His voice.

24. John 10:4.
25. Romans 12:2.

Pause and encounter

Ask Jesus:

Where am I in this picture?

Where are You calling me to be?

Am I just following the sheep in front of me?

Am I following the Shepherd?

Are my ears pricked to hear You?

I'm sorry for any way I have been following others and not listening for Your voice. Please help me to hear You and recognise Your voice.

Am I believing anything false that is blocking me from hearing Your voice?

I reject the false belief that . . .
(e.g. I can't hear You, You never speak to me)

What is the truth?

I receive the truth that . . .
(e.g. that You do want to speak to me)

Can things get in the way of us holding on to the truth He gives us? The book *Hinds' Feet on High Places*,[26] is an allegory that describes the journey of Much Afraid up to the High Places, to the Kingdom of Love. She has five enemies who follow her, who try to befriend her at her weakest moments, her vulnerable times. The enemies are named Self-Pity, Craven Fear, Bitterness, Resentment and Pride. Their voices can very easily drown out the voice of truth.

What are our enemies? What has settled comfortably into our thought life? What are our Achilles' heels, especially at our vulnerable times? Self-pity, fear and anxiety will try to rob us of hope and truth. We must jealously guard the truth, keeping a real check on our thought life. Seeking truth and feeding on truth helps fend off these enemies.

There are many times when I've got to the end of the day feeling a bit of a wobble or struggling and have really needed God to speak to me, to put things in the right perspective, to have His input on what is going on. So I simply ask, 'Please speak to me, I really need to hear.' Over and over again I have read something in the Bible, or in whichever book I'm drawn to, that has been so relevant and has brought peace and encouragement. Or whilst in prayer, a thought or image just drops into my mind that brings clarity. Often I go back through my notebook of things God has spoken to me. These have frequently been from other people receiving a word or image from God for me when praying together. Re-reading them has given me sustenance and encouragement.

---

26. Hannah Hurnard, *Hind's Feet on High Places* (Eastbourne: Kingsway Publications, 1995).

Treasuring His words, believing in His faithfulness, holding on to truth, all strengthen the hope that gets us through the night. His words of hope are like streetlights in the darkness. They give just enough light to guide us to the next streetlight, and then the next, and then the next, until . . . the dawn breaks.

Streetlights of hope lighting the way to the dawn.

> For we walk by faith, not by sight
> *2 Corinthians 5:7*

Pause and encounter

Ask Jesus:

Where am I in this picture?

Where am I fixing my gaze? (On the light? On the dark?)

What 'enemies' am I listening to?

Where am I not holding on to truth?

Please forgive me for fixing my gaze on . . . and for listening to the voices of . . . (e.g. fear, bitterness, resentment, self-pity . . .) Please help me to take my focus off these and onto Your truth and Your light.

What is the truth You want me to hold on to?

I choose to take hold of the truth that . . .

(e.g. nothing is too difficult for You, You have a way through this night, You are my provider, You love me and have this situation in Your hands)

Letting Go

Many things had to die in the desert. None of the Israelites who came out of Egypt reached the Promised Land: those who grumbled and complained, all the fighting men and those who worshipped idols. If we take the deaths symbolically, this was a purifying time. That inner fight, that inner resistance, that desire to do life our own way and by our own rules, has to die. We come to a place of surrender where we say, 'Your will be done.'

What of the 'idols' in our lives? All sorts of big and small 'idols' tempt us . . . The desire to have what 'everyone' else has, possessions, image, status, popularity, recognition, wealth . . . the list is endless.

This process of 'letting go' doesn't happen overnight. There is a time and place as we become ready to let go. It's often a process; we often can't do it all in one go. The more we see the Father's love, the more we see His tenderness and compassion and care, the more we grow in trust that His ways are good, the more these 'idols' lose their hold over us.

In *Hinds' Feet on High Places*,[27] when Much Afraid reaches the border of the high places of the Kingdom of Love, she is asked

---

27. Hurnard, *Hind's Feet on High Places*, pp. 132-136.

to lay down one of her desires on the altar. It is a truly painful time. She tries but she can't let go. She has to ask the Good Shepherd to do it for her, as it is beyond her own strength and ability. So, He reaches into her heart and tenderly and carefully untangles it from every part of her being and releases her from it. She is then immersed and drenched in peace. It was the right time to be released and now she is at rest and finally free. After a deep sleep she awakes to find herself in the most beautiful verdant spot by a pool. Immersing herself in the stream, it is as if she is soaking in waters of exuberant life. As she steps out of the stream, she has the most wonderful sense of happiness and vitality. She notices her feet are restored to perfection. She then sees her reflection in the pool and finds all the ugliness has gone and she is radiant with peace.

Shedding the old clothes, we find He is transforming us.

Pause and encounter

Ask Jesus:

Is there anything You are asking me to let go of?

Please help me have the strength and courage to let go of ... with Your help. I choose to let go of ... and I ask for Your help in letting go ... and I ask You to release me from the hold it has on me.

Is there any longing You are wanting me to put into Your hands?

I choose to place these longings into Your hands. I ask that You release me from their hold if this is not for me or the right time for me.

Are there any 'old clothes' I don't need to wear anymore?

I choose to give You the old clothes of ... and I choose not to wear them any longer. Please help me be released from them and take them from me.

What would You give me in exchange for letting go of these things?

I receive ... that You are giving instead ...

Unblocking the Spring

The film *Jean de Florette*[28] tells the story of a delightful man, Jean, and his wife inheriting a smallholding in the Pyrenees, a beautiful place. What Jean doesn't know is that his neighbours have discovered the quality of soil on his land is extremely good. They are jealous and want it for themselves, so they block up the spring on his land . . . and then befriend him.

He is full of enthusiasm and energy, ideas and passion for his smallholding. He plans to breed rabbits and grow their own food. It all starts very well . . . until the water in his cistern starts to run dry. He and his wife and daughter resort to going to a distant spring, trudging through the heat to bring back water. He works harder and harder, tries everything he can to turn around an increasingly desperate situation. All the time, the neighbours pretend to be helpful and friendly, but behind his back they are gleefully and evilly enjoying his suffering and defeat. Jean turns to drink in his desperation. Their resources have run dry, they have no money left and the rains haven't come. He angrily berates God for not bringing rain. Then, having driven himself into the ground, striving to make it all work, tragically, Jean dies.

---

28. *Jean de Florette*, distributed by Orion Pictures.

It's a heartrending and poignant film. There are broadly three approaches we can take to a challenging situation: give up and let it defeat us, do everything we can to fix it, or hold God's hand and find His route through it. Jean took the approach of striving in his own strength to fix the situation, putting more and more effort into it . . . until it killed him.

We can try to summon every bit of optimism and enthusiasm and positive thinking. We can work hard and try every possible self-help solution. But have we missed the fact that the spring is blocked and there is an evil one who is pleased?

There can be many 'false friends'.

- The false friend of 'self-sufficiency'?

- The false friend of 'serve and support everyone else but don't look after yourself'?

- The false friend of 'success, recognition and other people's praise proves everything is OK'?

- The false friend of 'try harder and don't be a burden on anyone else'?

- The false friend of 'don't appear weak or admit that you have needs'?

- The false friend of 'as long as I'm happy that's all that matters'?

- The false friend of 'everyone else is doing it, so it must be OK'?

We may have just been faithfully following those mindsets or cultural or family norms, believing that is the best and right way to live.

We may not realise that there is a spring, or if we do, that it is blocked; or that it can be unblocked. We may not realise that there can be a far greater flow of 'life', of 'living water'[29] in our lives. We think that this is our lot, this is just how we are, that this is 'our cross to bear'.

The stones blocking the spring can be anything that hinders the working of the Holy Spirit in our lives: unforgiveness, unbelief, a judgemental mindset, resentment, greed, stubbornness . . . anything that grieves the Holy Spirit.[30] The stones can also come from involvement in the wrong spiritual realm that is dark and not from God. Involvement in Freemasonry, the occult or New Age practices are other kinds of stones that can block the spring.

We need to ask God to expose and reveal the stones that are blocking the springs of living water in our lives, blocking the full flow of the Holy Spirit in and through us. We ask for revelation of not only the stones in our own lives, but also those that we have picked up from our family. We need to pray for God to expose what is hidden, to bring to light the strongholds we aren't aware of. Then, we need to ask God for forgiveness for each one.

The truth in *Jean de Florette* was that Jean had inherited a quality piece of land where he and his family could have thrived. The problem wasn't that God didn't send the rain; the problem wasn't that Jean hadn't tried hard enough; the problem was that the malicious neighbours had blocked the spring.

I remember at one point during the illness I saw this pattern of endless setbacks. I would recover from one very long virus and within a day or two I would be down with the next one, even

29.   John 4:10.
30.   Ephesians 4:30.

though I was extremely careful about where I went and washing hands, etc. Medical treatments that worked for others with similar diagnoses just didn't have as good a result with me. It felt like something fishy was going on. I very definitely then prayed for anything evil affecting my life to be exposed and brought into the light. The next day I received an email from a relative saying I might be interested in a relation, a few generations back, who had been well known in the United States. I explored her history, as there was quite a bit written about her. Yes, she was an interesting character, but there was a disturbing side to her and her father. She and her sister were both spiritualist mediums and their father ran a fraudulent hospice that profited from people's ill health.

I was well aware that engaging with the dark side brings bad consequences. Scripture states that Satan 'masquerades as an angel of light',[31] meaning that he can come across deceptively as good. He often makes dark things of his realm appealing and even appearing good or just harmless, in order to entice people in and entrap them, or gain a foothold in their lives. Opening the door to this realm can result in harmful repercussions on the family and even subsequent generations.

It is easy to see that family traits are also passed down the generations. Alcoholism, rage, low self-worth, being a workaholic, etc. is often passed from parent to child. Research has even found that trauma is passed down from parent to child.

We can also be affected by repercussions from an open door to the dark realm in the family line of spouses or previous partners. Yet God is a God of forgiveness and delights to set us free. He

---

31. 2 Corinthians 11:14.

can bring an end to the harmful consequences and the power of bad spiritual inheritance.

I have since seen many other people set free from oppression of one sort or another after removing the footholds of the adversary from their lives. Sometimes these things have come from their ancestors, or spouses, or previous partners; but sometimes they come from things they themselves have been involved in.

Freemasonry has a very definite effect on later generations, even though it appears innocuous at the entry levels. It is an example of the 'angel of light' at work. The oaths and prayers open the door to the dark side. I have seen people released from depression and illness after renouncing and breaking off the consequences of Freemasonry over their lives.

Other things like New Age healing practices, occult activities, séances, tarot cards, fortune telling etc., similarly give a foothold to the adversary and cause a stone to block the flow of the living water. Yet again, God sets us free when we walk away from and reject and renounce all allegiances to the dark realm, and ask for forgiveness and for Him to wash us clean and set us free.

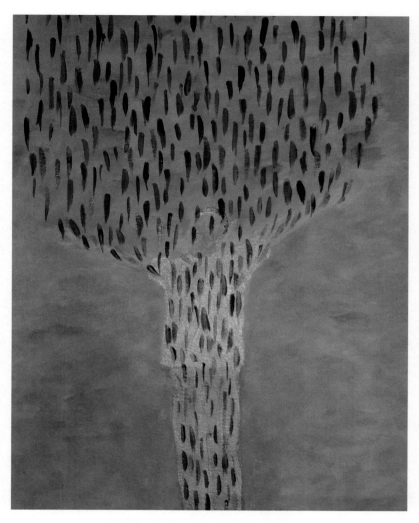

Unblocked spring of living water.

Pause and encounter

Ask Jesus:

What does the spring of living water look like in my life?

Are there any stones blocking its flow?

What are the names of the stones?

Are there any things I've been involved with or any attitudes that block the flow of Your life in me?

Please expose anything that is hidden that is affecting me.

I'm sorry for letting the stones of . . . into my life. Please forgive me for any way I have allowed them to be there. I am sorry for doing . . . and of attitudes of . . .

(I turn away from any involvement in New Age, witchcraft or occult activities. I renounce and break all allegiance and covenants and vows with Freemasonry or the occult that I have made knowingly or unknowingly, or my ancestors or any partners or their ancestors have made. I ask You to forgive me, wash me clean and set me free from any consequences in my life and to fill me with Your Holy Spirit instead.) *See Appendix 1 for more prayers.*

What 'enemy friends' (mindsets) have I been deceived by?

Please forgive me for mindsets of . . . (e.g. self-sufficiency, 'just be strong and carry on and don't ask for help', 'I will do life my own way' . . .)

I choose to walk away from these and I ask You to break their power from my life and set my free.

I forgive myself for doing and believing these things and I give all guilt and condemnation to You, Jesus. Please lift this off me in Your mercy. Thank You that You died for everything I have done wrong in thought or deed, so that I can be forgiven.

Our View of God

The story of Jean de Florette also sadly highlights how we can blame God, how our hearts can harden towards Him, because we have interpreted our situation incorrectly. Totally understandably, Jean de Florette was desperate, he had tried everything he could, so why couldn't God have sent the rain? Why couldn't God have had compassion?

It is so easy for us to misinterpret our pain, misinterpret our struggles and conclude, consciously or unconsciously, that God doesn't really care, that He doesn't really love us. We may think, 'Yes, He may love everyone else, but He seems to have overlooked me', or, 'I am not worthy of His love, I am not that important.' We may think that we have been overlooked time and time again by other people, and come to the conclusion that that's 'just who we are', it's our lot. We see it as a reflection of our worth.

Jesus said that it is the *truth* that sets us free.[32] The truth would have set Jean free. Had Jean seen the deeds for his land, he would have seen that he *owned* a spring! Had Jean been discerning regarding his neighbours, rather than being deceived, if he had found the spring and unblocked it, he and his family could have lived in the abundance of a rich inheritance and thrived. His heart would not have hardened towards God.

---

32. John 8:32.

Perhaps some of the biggest challenges along the desert route are not to let our hearts harden towards God, not to let disillusionment and disappointment take hold, and not to let a chasm grow between God and ourselves – a chasm from our pain. We may not notice a gradual hardening of our hearts, but a subtle shift against God can develop. In our minds, we may be holding on to a belief that God is good, yet our hearts are carrying pain which is growing seeds of anger, unbelief or resentment towards Him. Or in our minds, we may have decided that God doesn't care, yet our hearts are crying out for His love. Walls and barriers and distance can begin to become established.

From leading many inner healing prayer sessions, I have seen over and over again people carrying a view of God as being an angry God, a distant God, one who doesn't have time for them, one who doesn't know them, one who doesn't care for them, one who doesn't understand them. So often this has come directly from their experience of their earthly father, which they have projected onto God.

It is a view that is very, very far from the truth.

> And I pray that you, being rooted
> and established in love,
> may have power,
> together with all the Lord's people,
> to grasp how wide and long and high and deep
> is the love of Christ,
> and to know this love that surpasses knowledge –
> that you may be filled to the measure
> of all the fullness of God.
>
> *Ephesians 3:17-19*

Pause and encounter

Ask Father God:

Is there anything I am believing about You, Father God, that is not true?

I reject the false belief that God . . .

(e.g. is distant, doesn't really love me, isn't able to help and provide, is always angry)

Is there anything I need to forgive my own father for?

If you are able . . . Dad, today I choose to forgive you for . . . and for the consequences this has had on my life . . . and for all the ways you weren't there for me or able to give me what I needed. I cancel all 'debts' I have felt you have owed me.

What is the truth about You, Father God?

I receive the truth that God is . . .

Father God, please show what Your love for me looks like.

Repeat this for your mother, as issues and unmet needs in this area can often affect our view of and connection with the Holy Spirit.

(God encompasses a mother and father heart towards us as God is beyond gender – male and female are made in the image of God, see Genesis 1:27.)

Time for Healing

Over the years we may have pushed down our pain, tried to ignore it and move on, but time on its own doesn't heal. We may have built up a pressure cooker of emotional stress and hurts, or we may have pushed them down so deep we almost aren't aware they are there, but our body and soul are carrying them, and being harmed. God loves us far too much to let us stay in that place.

He is longing to bring His gentle healing touch to release us from the traumas that we are carrying, the griefs and pains that we have buried. We need His love to melt and heal the scars that may have built a wall of 'protection', a shield or hardness around our hearts. We may have carried these hurts for so long, or buried them so deep, or looked for comfort in all the wrong places, that maybe now, in the challenges of the desert, it is time for them to come to the surface and be healed.

To receive emotional healing, it is so helpful to meet with Jesus in those areas where we are stuck. We need to grieve, we need to be real with our emotions, honest about the anger and disappointment and the very real pain we carry. Yet we don't want to be stuck there. We need to encounter healing in those places.

It can be helpful, from a place of feeling Jesus with you, to return to those times of pain and disappointment, and encounter Jesus there in those memories. We can ask Jesus to lift the pain off us, for Him to carry it, and then actively release our pain to Him. We can ask Him for the truth He wants to speak to us there. (If they are very traumatic memories, or you have post-traumatic stress disorder, only do this with someone trained in this, and only if Jesus wants to take you there now – He may want to do other healing first. He may want to bring healing in a different way.) He does want to heal and is able to take the pain and trauma out of all our painful memories and bring healing to us. It is like He rewrites those memories, even if we didn't know Him at the time. He wants to carry the pain for us and bring truth to our ways of interpreting what has happened. He is there to lift the shame off us and exchange it for His immense, unconditional love, healing and peace.

From a place of seeing our past painful situations with Jesus in those memories, with Jesus carrying our pain, with His perspective on those who caused us grief . . . we need to release the bitterness and unforgiveness towards those people. We need to forgive them in order to set ourselves free. We need to let go of our judgements towards them and hand them over to Father God for Him to be their judge and their healer. Perhaps we need to let go of bitterness towards God? Maybe we need to forgive ourselves?

Releasing the pain to Jesus.

For myself, there had been a struggle in my heart to really feel that God cared about how long I had been ill. I knew it in my head and had seen over and over again how He had provided work for me almost miraculously, or had spoken to me just when I needed it, or provided a new friendship at just the right time. He had looked after me in many other ways, especially at my most difficult times. I had seen His provision and evidence of His love repeatedly and absolutely knew that He was right there with me in the journey. However, with my health, the buffeting had been relentless, long, with endless setbacks and pretty rough at times . . . so there had been a struggle to feel that He truly cared.

A breakthrough came for me during an Art Sozo[33] ministry session. (This is where you can encounter God and healing through using paint to express your emotions, and express the emotions connected to what you are hearing from God.) I made a decision to be real and honest with how I was feeling as I painted and it unlocked some very deep pain in this area and brought it to the surface with many tears. That is when God spoke. He gently said, 'I knew this would be hard, but I knew you could do it.' Along with this, there was the sense that He was so proud of me, a Father's heart of deep compassion and care towards His daughter. There was the sense that of course He had held my hand, walked with me and even carried me through it all, but that He had been proud of my part in it, of me getting through it with Him. This dissolved all sense that He didn't care and just opened up an awareness of a huge heart beating with love for me. Along with this, there was the sense of unspoken words that it must be so worth it; that He wouldn't have allowed such a challenging route if there hadn't been a very good reason for it and with very real riches and treasures to come from it. It hasn't answered the 'why?' but He said, 'Trust Me, it's so worth it.'

He then said, 'This has been your death, but also your resurrection.'

---

33.   www.artsozo.com (accessed 13.8.21).

The chasm of pain, causing a gulf between us and Father God.

Encountering Jesus in our pain.

The chasm healed and transformed to gold.
In the Father's embrace.

Pause and encounter

Ask Jesus:

Is there any pain in my life that You want me to give You to carry now?

Imagine the pain as an object you can give to Jesus, then hand it to Jesus saying . . . Jesus, I don't want to carry this pain any longer. I give it to You. Please take it from me . . . and show me what You are doing with it . . .

What would You give me in exchange?'

If you are feeling Jesus is with you, then ask . . . Is there any memory You want to take me to and bring healing to?

Where are You, Jesus, in this memory? *If you can't sense Him there, ask Him to come into the memory.*

Jesus, what are You doing or saying?

What wrong interpretation did I make in that situation? What did I start to believe that isn't true?

What is the truth?

I give the pain in this memory to You now. I don't want to carry it any longer. Please lift it from me. *Imagine yourself giving the pain to Jesus.*

Please show me what You are now doing in that situation.

Is there anything else You want to say to me here?

Is there anyone I need to forgive (including myself)?

I ask You to help me forgive . . . and I choose to forgive them for what they did and the consequences on my life. Please help me see them through Your eyes.

Death and Resurrection

The principle of death and resurrection runs through the Bible. The concept is that out of 'dying', power and much greater abundant life is released. Jesus used the analogy of a grain of wheat falling into the ground and dying. Without its own death, it cannot produce a harvest.[34] The fundamental expression of this is the death and resurrection of Jesus Himself. His death released the resurrection power of the Holy Spirit to become available to all believers. His death provided the ultimate sacrifice for all the wrong in us.

As with all of God's principles, it is the deeper inner experience that is key. An inner dying to 'self' releases God's resurrection power in our lives. An inner dying does not mean hope dying or disillusionment setting in, or giving up. Far from it. It is a yielding to God. It is a dying to our own lives, in order to receive His life within us. Rather than being destroyed, it is being made new. It is having each area of our life submitted to His lordship. Without us in the way, He is able to work powerfully through us.

As we die to things such as self-centredness, our own agenda and wanting to do things our way, we break the power of the adversary in our life. Temptations have less and less of a hold, as those areas of our life come under God's lordship.

---

34.   John 12:24.

Our motives get purified. Through the 'dying' we transition from it being about us, to delighting to do what God wants. We move away from self-focus and selfish ambition; doing things for our fulfilment, or to look better, or to be noticed, or to get attention. We move to a place of saying yes to things simply because God has asked us to. It comes from a purified motive of obedience and delighting to do His will. We say 'no' to things if He says 'no'. It's no longer about our reputation and pleasing others; it is about His glory and pleasing Him.

We are not being annihilated; rather, we are coming to true life. The grey colours of the 'self-life' give way to the vibrant colours of Christ within us. As we let go, resurrection life can come in. We actually become more of our true selves, because we become free.

> God has chosen to make known . . . the
> glorious riches of this mystery,
> which is Christ in you,
> the hope of glory.
>
> *Colossians 1:27*

I remember seeing a picture of a tree that had fallen over but still had its roots in the ground and had re-sprouted. It powerfully touched my spirit. The tree hadn't given up, even though it had gone through a great storm. New life had grown from within it. I felt led to paint a similar scene. As I painted, further aspects evolved. There were axe wounds in the trunk, which were leaking golden sap. The tree was bathed in God's love, and this love was soaking into every wound.

I researched what happens with wounds in a tree trunk. Interestingly, they are a place where disease can enter, as well as where sap can leak out. Depending on the nature of the tree, the sap can be sweet or not so sweet. It also seemed as I painted the picture that the wounds were entry points where God's love could soak in more deeply than in any other part of the tree. There is a vulnerability and openness there. The thick bark does not get in the way.

Through the 'deaths' and the wounds, God's life can soak in deep, as long as we don't let the disease of bitterness enter instead. He helps us to live again in a whole new way. The sap, His fragrance, can also emerge from within us, pure and sweet, through the very wounds that inflicted the pain.

We must not mistake 'dying to ourselves' to mean we don't matter. It doesn't mean we disconnect from our needs, our emotions and our body. In Philippians, Paul says 'my God will meet all your needs according to the riches of his glory in Christ Jesus'.[35] Our needs really matter to Him.

We can be focused on trying to do the right thing and doing what we think God is asking, but actually living from our minds and not being truly in touch with ourselves. We can be loving and serving others, but not loving ourselves. We can be ignoring what our bodies are trying to tell us and ignoring the build-up of emotional stress. This is not dying to ourselves; this is being out of touch with and not looking after the person God created and loves deeply.

The *'dying'* needs to be seen in the context of being *raised* up with Christ. It's far from being dead. It's a gateway to living a resurrection life.

---

35. Philippians 4:19.

*Resurrection growth and golden sap
pouring from the fallen tree.*

We were therefore buried with him
through baptism into death
in order that, just as Christ was raised from the
dead through the glory of the Father,
we too may live a new life.

Romans 6:4

Intimacy with God

Through Moses, God ordained three main festivals for the Israelite people. These were Passover in the first month, Pentecost in the third month and Tabernacles in the seventh month. It can be helpful to look at what these three festivals point to, at how they can have a fulfilment in our own lives.

The Passover festival remembered the time when God delivered the Israelites from centuries of slavery in Egypt; the time when they had to put the blood of a sacrificed lamb on the doorposts of their houses to be spared from the judgement on Egypt.

The festival of Passover has a perfect spiritual fulfilment in the death of Jesus on the cross, being the once-and-for-all sacrifice for sins. Jesus actually said when breaking the bread and taking the cup of wine at the Passover meal, to 'do this in remembrance of me'.[36]

So the fulfilment of Passover in our own lives is seen in us leaving behind our 'Egypt', representing our old life, in exchange for a new life with God. The Passover represents the open way for us to be freed from inner slavery, by turning away from a life not submitted to God, and receiving forgiveness for our wrongdoings, through the death of Jesus.

---

36.   Luke 22:19.

Fulfilment of the festival of Pentecost is our infilling with the Holy Spirit. At Pentecost, following the crucifixion of Jesus, the Holy Spirit was poured out on the new believers in Jerusalem.[37] This infilling of the Holy Spirit began a total transformation in these people. It led to a time of community in the body of believers, and a release of the gifts of the Holy Spirit to build them up and encourage them. These gifts included prophecy, speaking in tongues, and gifts of healing and miracles.[38]

Pentecost at the time of Moses, then known as the Festival of Weeks, marked the grain harvest. This mirrors the inner reality that infilling of the Holy Spirit is so essential for spiritual fruitfulness and harvest in our lives. It provides the power to live this new life with Christ.

We can be stuck at either Passover or Pentecost, just content with Passover, that we are forgiven and in God's family; or focused on Pentecost, pursuing the gifts and power of the Holy Spirit and meeting together. Both of these are essential, but there is more.

So what of the third festival, Tabernacles (or Sukkot, meaning booths)? During the Tabernacles festival, the Israelites were to celebrate the ingathering of the full harvest. They were also to live in temporary shelters to remind them of their time of coming out of Egypt, living in the desert as they journeyed to the Promised Land.

The Day of Atonement precedes this festival by a few days. This was a time of purifying of the sins of the previous year. Aaron, the high priest, would perform sacrifices for the forgiveness of these sins and then he would go into the Holy of Holies before the Lord.[39]

---

37. Acts 2:1-4.
38. 1 Corinthians 12:9-11.
39. Leviticus 16.

So, Tabernacles celebrated the full harvest but also reminded the Israelites of their time in the wilderness. It followed the purification time of the Day of Atonement. This festival has different aspects, and is fulfilled in a variety of ways.

We experience the beginning of the harvest in the fulfilment of Pentecost, when we receive the Holy Spirit into our lives; but the full harvest does not come until the fulfilment of Tabernacles.

In many ways, our inner journey through the wilderness into the full harvest time of the Promised Land is our own fulfilment of Tabernacles. The journey through the wilderness brings the wrong in us to the surface. To enter the Promised Land the Israelites had to cross the river Jordan. Just as the purifying time of the Day of Atonement preceded Tabernacles, there is similar imagery of going through the Jordan, like a baptism, for our deep cleansing, before coming into the fullness of the Promised Land.

We received forgiveness for the wrong in us as we came to Jesus in our 'Passover' experience. We then need to walk forward into the reality of breaking free of those wrong powers, being purified and becoming changed people, maybe partly through a wilderness experience.

Anyone who went into the Holy of Holies with any sin in them would die. So only Aaron the high priest could go in, and only after making special sacrifices, washing himself and wearing holy robes. Considering the awesome fearfulness of this situation, it is incredible that at the moment Jesus died (as the ultimate sacrifice for sins), the veil of the temple was torn in two; the way had been made open for us ourselves to come into the presence of God.[40]

40. Mark 15:38; Hebrews 10:19.

As we are cleansed and changed, we can come into the presence of God in a deeper and deeper way. Aaron came before God alone. So unlike the Pentecost experience of communal moving in the gifts and power of the Holy Spirit, this has an additional focus on us alone with God. In beautiful solitude, we can draw close to the loving Father heart of God.

We move into the Tabernacles celebration of the full harvest, the season of the Promised Land.

A sanctuary in the desert, solitude with Father God.

The concept of solitude and coming close to the heart of God may be challenging. We may find barriers hindering us from drawing close to God. We can feel unworthy, that God is too busy, or wouldn't be interested in us, or we've failed too many times. These are all lies. He forgives, He loves and He washes us clean. He longs to spend time with us.

As the heavy cloaks of unworthiness and condemnation are lifted off us, we find it easier to open our hearts to God. As the distorting lenses we view God through are removed, we begin to let Him draw close. We open up to His healing; the love that heals our souls. His love starts to invade every broken area and every area of shame. His encouragement and the Father's heart towards us envelop and nurture the areas of dormant potential within us. The fullness of our true self begins to emerge. As we let His love in, we grow in accepting and embracing ourselves. We begin to feel and know in our hearts that we are a cherished child of God. We no longer take our view of ourselves from how we are or were received by others, or through the filter of wounds from the past. We experience more of His true nature of love. We have the dawning of a realisation that we are His beloved. We come to a place of rest. We come home.

My beloved spoke and said to me,
'Arise, my love, my beautiful one, come with me.'
Song of Songs 2:10

At rest

Pause and encounter

Ask Father God:

Is there anything blocking me coming into Your presence?

If an attitude or behaviour is highlighted, try to choose to walk away from it with God's help.

Please forgive me for . . . I receive Your forgiveness and I forgive myself. I ask for Your strength to walk away from this and live the life You have called me to.

Is there anything I am believing about myself that is preventing me from drawing close to you?

I reject the false belief that I am . . .

What is the truth?

I receive the truth that I am . . .

Is there any way I have rejected myself?

Please forgive me for not accepting and embracing how You have made me. Please help me to love myself and love how You have made me.

Do I have any false belief about the way You see me?

I reject the belief that You . . .

Father God, how do You see me?

Father God, what does Your love for me look like?

Worship

I had quite a profound experience with one of my first attempts at painting with the Holy Spirit. As a piece of beautiful, worshipful music was playing, I found myself being drawn into painting the experience of worshipping God. It started with painting the flow of worship going up towards God and, as that increased, the presence of God started to rain down. God's presence alighted upon the worshipper, causing them to glow and be tinged with His glory. This increased the flow of worship towards God. More and more of His glory and His presence fell, both in the painting and upon me. It became like being on holy ground. It was a beautiful, glorious, almost electric presence. I was soaking and bathing in it. The whole atmosphere changed. Then to my surprise, I was so clearly drawn to paint fire igniting on the earth around. It was as if God's presence came to such a level that fire spontaneously fanned into flame. His power was being released to earth by the worship.

When the disciples asked Jesus how to pray, in saying, 'Our Father in heaven, hallowed be your name',[41] Jesus was giving the first principle, the starting place. He wasn't prescribing a ritual of words to repeat. He was showing where our hearts needed

---

41. Matthew 6:9.

to be. He was effectively saying to honour and bow down before the true nature of God. This should come first. He wasn't saying, 'Start with presenting your requests or needs to God.' He was saying, 'Put God on the throne, not your problems.' This is the nature of worship: our hearts enthroning God in our life. It is inwardly bowing before Him. It is revering and lifting up the truth that His ways are far higher, far greater, far more loving and far more powerful than we can ever realise in this lifetime.

We may not feel this right now, or even believe it. Yet choosing to start from this place can shift the atmosphere around us. It can shift the discouragement, the low mood, or the fear. It can release God's presence to come. It dethrones the problem, it dethrones the fear, it dethrones the lies and unbelief. If God's presence doesn't come right away, let's persevere until it does.

As we worship from the heart, His presence falls.

Pause and encounter

Try and pray from the heart along the lines of:

'Lord God I thank You that You are Lord over all. You are love. You set the captives free. You are an almighty God; You are truth; You are the provider of all our needs.

'Your power is greater than anything else at work over my life. Your love for me is greater than any other love I will ever experience. Your peace is way above every fear and anxiety at work in the world, and beyond understanding. Your healing is greater than any other I could ever experience. Your ways are higher than our ways.* Your wisdom is far greater than ours.

'Nothing is impossible for You. I choose You as Lord over my life and my situation. Nothing else can sit on that throne. I love You, I worship You.'

Then spend some time thanking God for anything you can.

Let your heart rise up to God, maybe through music that is worshipful.

Try to worship God from the heart, through prayer or song or in stillness.

*From Isaiah 55:9

The Cosmic War

In the fictional film *Life Is Beautiful*,[42] a delightful Jewish family with a young son are imprisoned in a concentration camp during the Second World War. It's a beautiful story of the father's love doing everything he can to protect his son from the reality of the concentration camp. The father pretends that it's a big game and that if the boy follows all the rules carefully he will get to ride in a tank at the end. It's a tender story of the father protecting the boy from the full realities of the war and the boy simply trusting his father, believing him and obeying him at every turn. The boy's trust and obedience saves his life. The father's deep love and protection shield his son, providing security and safety, despite the reality around him.

There is a poignant scene towards the end of the film when the war is nearly over. The Allies are on their way, but the boy has to hide in a box overnight and wait and wait until the soldiers leave, before he can come out. There is a very tense time when a guard dog sniffs him out, but it's the boy's absolute trust in his father that enables him to wait and obey through an incredibly difficult time, perhaps for him the darkest hour before the dawn. Then follows the most beautiful moment, he emerges from the

---

42. *Life Is Beautiful*, distributed by Cecchi Gori Group (Italy) and Miramax Films (USA/ International).

box, after the occupying soldiers have left and the concentration camp has been liberated, to find a huge Allies' tank coming round the corner. The tank that his father had promised him! His face is radiant as he cries, 'It was true.' The promise he had held on to and trusted through such a long and difficult time, had come true. And the 'game' was over.

What had the boy done to be caught up in this war, to be in the concentration camp? Nothing, other than being true to his identity. He was Jewish and the enemy didn't like him.

Conflict and struggles can also be directly due to the adversary coming against God birthing something new and powerful. When Moses was born, Pharaoh ordered all the Israelite baby boys to be killed. Moses was only saved because his mother hid him in a basket in the bulrushes by the river, where he was rescued by an Egyptian princess.[43] When Jesus was born, Herod also ordered all the boys under two to be killed, in order to try to kill Jesus. So Joseph and Mary had to flee with Him to Egypt.[44] So, a big conflict going on in our lives may mean God is birthing something significant. What may seem an enormous discouragement may be a huge encouragement in disguise. God is on the move.

There is a cosmic war going on; there is an evil one who hates us. Yet, there is a Father God who is always there to carry us through, to give us hope, to protect us, to guide us, to love us. It is so key to trust Him; to listen for His voice and obey Him, to survive this war. We have a very real adversary. We need to be wise and aware.

---

43. Exodus 2:1-10.
44. Matthew 2:13-18.

When I reached seven years of being ill, I hit a low point of crushing disappointment. I suppose my hope had been that maybe seven years would be it. Seven years is a good number with God, meaning perfection and completion, so hopefully, this would be it. But no. During a moment of a real pouring out of my pain, disappointment and crushed hopes to God, I had a very clear picture in my mind of a sword driven right into the middle of my back. The obvious meaning was that the thief, the destroyer was trying to take me out. So asking God what to do with this, I saw the sword being taken out of my back and put into my hand – a very bright shining sword. What had tried to come against me, to 'steal and kill and destroy'[45] was being turned instead into a strength, a gift and something of power.

Equipped.

45. John 10:10.

You intended to harm me,
but God intended it for good . . .

Genesis 50:20

The Thief

A friend had a prophetic dream where a burglar had a key to the front door of her house. During the night the burglar calmly and confidently walked in and stole whatever he wanted, and came back for more. Her valuable, precious belongings were steadily removed.

A very pertinent dream. Significantly, there was no need for hand-to-hand combat with the thief. However, she now needed to change the locks and not give away the key again, removing the opportunity for the thief to enter and steal.

Wherever the thief has a key or an open door, he will rob us very happily and come back for more. We cannot just accept ongoing theft. It is crucial to ask God to show us where we have given the thief permission to enter our lives, where he has a legal right, where we have given him a key, where the doors are open. For example, if we have wrong beliefs – such as God just wants us to suffer – or if we have wrong behaviour or attitudes, we give the thief the right to rob us.

It can also be as if we have a monkey sitting on our shoulder whispering into our ear and pointing things out to us. Maybe a monkey called Discouragement who likes to point out what we are missing out on. It likes to pretend it is our best friend, who really understands what we are feeling; stroking our hair and saying 'what a bad time you're having' and 'it's not fair' and 'God can't really care'. Or perhaps it's a monkey called Despair or a monkey called Disappointment or a monkey called Fear or Anxiety or Negativity or Be Critical. It keeps feeding our thoughts with its whisperings . . . those thoughts that actually come from the adversary and ignore God's perspective, but can seem very true. Meanwhile, the atmosphere over us has become heavy, has got oppressive and the not-so-friendly monkey has pickpocketed us and robbed us of our joy, leaving a cloud of gloom, which is hard to see through with any clarity.

> The thief comes only to steal and kill and destroy;
> I have come that they may have life,
> and have it to the full.
>
> *John 10:10*

Doors to the thief firmly closed,
safe in the strong tower of God's protection.

Along with wrong mindsets, unforgiveness and strongholds in us, our heart is a very vulnerable area where we can open a door to the thief.

> Watch over your heart with all diligence,
> For from it flow the springs of life.
>
> *Proverbs 4:23, NASB*

In *The Passion Translation* this reads as:

> *So above all, guard the affections of your heart*
> *for they affect all that you are.*
> *Pay attention to the welfare of your innermost being,*
> *for from there flows the wellspring of life.*

In the Bible, both the Greek and Hebrew words for 'heart' encompass the inner person, the mind, the will and the seat of the emotions. Temptations of all sorts will assail us, subtle or not so subtle. The thief is very aware of our vulnerabilities. He is skilled at trying to entice us down wrong avenues . . . which then leave our 'front doors' open.

When we know we are trying just a bit too hard to justify our actions, when we are not willing to bring an area of our lives before God, alarm bells should start to ring. As we let wrong attachments into our hearts, the wellsprings of life start to dry up; they hinder the flow and life of the Holy Spirit in us and the true joy that comes from Him.

It can be so hard to let go and walk away from these enticements of the heart, but God is the Comforter, the Restorer and the Healer of our hearts. He is the God of exchange for the better. As we shut the door to what is eroding the true life within, He opens the way to the best, to what truly meets the desires of our hearts, the desires He has put there, that genuinely give life to who we are.

> Delight yourself in the LORD;
> And He will give you the desires of your heart
> *Psalm 37:4, NASB*

Pause and encounter

Ask Jesus:

Is there a door open in my life allowing the thief to enter?

Is there anything I need to turn away from?

With things that come to mind, ask for forgiveness and try to make a choice to want to stop/change/move on . . . asking for the power of the Holy Spirit to help.

Is there any 'monkey' that I'm listening to?

Is there anything false that I'm believing that is allowing that 'monkey' to stay?

I reject the belief that . . .

I choose to turn away from feeding on disappointment/ negativity/ fear/discouragement/despair. I give You those feelings and I now choose to refuse to listen to those voices. I command discouragement/despair/fear/negativity to leave me in Jesus' name. I ask You, Jesus, that You feed me with Your promises and Your hope and Your truth. I ask that You give me discernment in what I am listening to in my thoughts.

Have I opened up my heart to any wrong things?

Please help me to have the courage and strength to make the right choices. Help to let go of what I need to let go of, and please break its hold on me. Please forgive me for where I have . . .

I want to put my heart into Your hands for You to cleanse it and fill it with desires from You.

Healthy Emotions and Standing Tall

Some of the suffering we go through can be directly attributed to other people's actions. How do we handle this well? Christian teaching hasn't always had the healthiest or maybe most balanced approach to our *emotional* journey. If the main message is just to forgive, turn the other cheek, love our enemies[46] and not trust our emotions . . . what do we do with the difficult emotions? And how does that leave us feeling about ourselves?

Romans 8:21 talks about the 'glorious freedom of God's children',[47] which God is bringing about. This includes 'glorious freedom' in our emotions; not the freedom to act in whatever way we feel like, but a glorious inner well-being.

We want to do right, show grace and God's love to everyone, be forgiving, coming alongside the 'unlovely', and be self-controlled. But we get hurt, we get battered, and we do forgive . . . but how well are we dealing with the hurt, the anger and the consequences?

It is the message of 'religion' that you just have to behave right; but when others inflict suffering on us, God wants to help us

---

46. Luke 6:27-29.
47. Romans 8:21, ISV.

navigate it in a wholesome way. Yes, forgiveness is essential, but it doesn't stand alone; God loves the whole person and wants to walk us through the processing of suffering in an *emotionally healthy way*.

How we *think* about situations can affect how we *feel*. So healthy emotions will come from healthy thinking.[48] If we look out of the window, see grey skies and think this is going to be a miserable day, it's very likely we will feel miserable. So when we have difficult emotions, they don't necessarily reflect the truth, but we need to understand why they are there. They are warning lights, indicating that something needs processing, or addressing, or healing.

A healthy way of processing difficult emotions looks for the gift they bring;[49] the highlighting of what needs addressing, or the motivation for action. They can be a red flag for what needs to change and an impetus to pray and act. But we should also be seeking a truthful, objective evaluation of the situation and looking for God's perspective.

There is clinical evidence to suggest that a denial, repression, or lack of processing emotions can lead to depression, physical pain, back pain, migraines or fatigue.[50] We may need to look at this area quite carefully, rather than always assume there is solely a physical or medical cause.

Let's look at a few ways of responding to conflict:

---

48. Cognitive behavioural therapy is based on the idea that our thoughts can affect our feelings and our behaviour.
49. Chip Dodd, *The Voice of the Heart: A Call to Full Living* (Tampa, FL: Sage Hill, 2015).
50. John Sarno, *The Mindbody Prescription* (New York: Hachette Book Group, 1999). Note: I don't necessarily agree with all his views, in particular on Lyme disease.

Some people focus inward and blame themselves. When other people have mistreated them, they carry the shame. They don't feel the injustice, only false guilt.

Other people will deflect all focus from themselves and blame others instead. To avoid looking at their own needs for growth, they project their own issues onto other people, often with uncalled-for anger. Anger towards others can often be used to hide or protect oneself from a more vulnerable emotion.

Yet others take the approach of being strong; it's water off a duck's back; they move on as if it's not a big deal, but sometimes this is a form of denial and suppression of emotion and the water is actually seeping into the duck's back, and they carry the tension and stress in their bodies instead.

I wonder: what is our default response?

Jesus had healthy emotions. He wept, He got angry with the desecration of the temple, He needed to withdraw and have space and time alone with the Father, He was able to speak the truth with love and no fear.

Here are some questions that maybe worth considering:

- Do I have a build-up of emotional stress, of things that I am not dealing with, just pushing down?

- Am I overreacting? Is there underlying pain that needs healing?

- Do I seek God for what is the truth, before I react?

- Am I seeking God's wisdom and His perspective when handling conflict?

- When I have forgiven and know that I am forgiven, do I then stand tall?

- Do I allow myself to have appropriate anger when I need to?[51]

- Do I allow myself to cry and release an emotional build-up to God?

- Am I just trying to do what's right and not listening to red flags in my emotions?

- Am I allowing enough time to draw aside and hear the true voice of the Lord?

- Am I being swept along by my own enthusiasm and not checking to see if I am really on the track God wants?

- Am I being led by my emotions and ignoring the 'check' or disquiet in my spirit?

- Is there any shame or false guilt that I'm carrying that I need to give to God?

- Am I able to receive God's love and forgiveness?

Let's take a healthy route with processing our emotions. We need to connect with them honestly and take them to God. We may find our thinking doesn't align with His perspective and that He wants to speak truth to us. We may discover that earlier memories come to the surface and we see a pattern emerging, showing a need for deeper healing. We may find we have been just reacting from our emotions, maybe impulsively, but not going that step further to seek how God is wanting us respond.

51. Ephesians 4:26.

In facilitating inner healing prayer sessions, I have found it can be extremely helpful for the guest to ask God how He sees the person who has mistreated them. So often people have then seen their abuser as a scared little boy who had a very angry father, or someone who is bowed over and deeply full of shame. Standing in the abuser's shoes or understanding a bit more of what the abuser was dealing with can make it much easier to forgive.

So let's be careful when we forgive, that we are first being emotionally honest and healthy. We need to be seeing the situation and ourselves in the right light, with truth. We need to break agreement with anything that has tried to push us down and condemn us, so that we can stand tall. Then let's forgive, to set ourselves free. God can then give us His love for our 'enemies'.[52]

'Negative' emotions in their right place have a healthy role. They are there to process grief, keep us safe and motivated for what needs to change. However, when these dominate or get out of control they become a stronghold in us. If we take these strongholds to God, their power can be broken. He can show us the root of how they took hold. There can be many causes. We may be carrying unforgiveness, unhealed trauma, an inherited generational trait, a wrongdoing or attitude to ask forgiveness for, a false belief about God, an opened door to the dark realm etc. – all of which He loves to forgive, heal and bring us freedom from.

Another danger is that we judge others through bitterness or hurt. As Jesus said, 'For in the same way as you judge others, you will be judged, and with the measure you use, it will be

52. Luke 6:35.

measured to you.[53] We reap what we sow.[54] Cycles of hurt and offence can repeat. We need to discern what is right and wrong, but not stand as judge over the people involved. We don't stand in their shoes or know what they may be dealing with, or the strongholds of the adversary they are battling with. We may be viewing them through our own filters.

I have seen a variety of examples of this, where people have made judgements of others, and have then had to deal with the same affliction or circumstances themselves. Often after repenting of the judgement and forgiving those they had judged, the affliction has ceased. We don't realise the consequences of judging others, of how it can set up a reaping of the same thing in our own lives.

So let's bring our whole emotional life before God and how we react to difficult behaviour in others. Let's find a way of processing our emotions with God; not repressing them but being real before Him; finding a truthful perspective, and responding in a healthy way.

A pertinent example of acting on emotions without God is the outburst of anger of the young Moses at the injustice he saw over his people the Israelites – in slavery. The anger was healthy. The oppression, injustice and cruelty against his people was immense and completely undeserved. He then took his anger out on an Egyptian and killed him.[55] He directed his anger in the wrong place. The Egyptian was obeying his orders; he was under the control of Pharaoh. He wasn't the source of the problem and killing him certainly didn't help. Yet God had planted that righteous indignation and passion in Moses and that was the

---

53. Matthew 7:2.
54. See Galatians 6:7.
55. Exodus 2:11-12.

beginning of his call to set his people free. He had to learn to do it God's way; when his heart was in the right place; and when he was prepared and equipped by God to lead them out of slavery.

So let's pursue the 'glorious freedom of God's children';[56] with the beautiful inner well-being of a healthy emotional life, humbly standing tall in the Father's absolute acceptance, love and grace.

Shedding the shame and standing tall.

---

56.   Romans 8:21, ISV.

Pause and encounter

Ask Jesus:

Is there anything that has come over me or against me that I need to have a healthy emotional response to?

It may help to write an honest letter and then burn it, or express your feelings to God.

Please show me what I need to reject and break agreement with and what I need to come out from being under.

I break agreement with control/condemnation/shame/false guilt/being put down/. . . and I ask You Jesus to set me free from their hold on me . . . I choose to come out from under it.

When I have been hurt by others, what wrong interpretations have I made?

What is the truth?

Jesus, how do You see me?

Jesus, how do You see them?

I receive this truth, and from a place of standing tall in Your freedom, forgiveness and grace, I now choose to forgive . . .

Have I made any judgements towards this person?

I am sorry for judging them and assuming I know why they did what they did. I ask that You now break the cycle of sowing and reaping and cancel out the consequences of my judgement.

Freedom

Through the knocks of life, we can gradually build a wall around us as a protection from further hurt. We can add a new stone with each new betrayal, or broken trust, or hurtful word. Each time we vow 'I will never let that happen to me again' the wall grows. Each time we let a wound fester and are not quick to forgive, we add another stone. Whenever we judge others and assume we know their motives, we add to the wall between others and ourselves. When disappointment sinks deep, we can add to a protective wall of low expectation. When we don't understand tragedy and we blame God, we build a wall between us and God. When our emotions are too hard to bear or feel too shameful, we can build a wall within ourselves to shut them out.

When we are young, these walls between us and other people can help us cope. In situations of abuse and neglect, the walls to shut out the difficult emotions can be vital for survival. But there comes a time when we are ready for the walls to come down. As our inner selves are healed and we receive truth, the walls are no longer serving a helpful purpose and are holding us back from a full life. The walls keep us from true connection with God, or with others, or with ourselves.

These defences can manifest in different ways. We can keep people at a distance by not risking being open and vulnerable.

Being critical, judgemental or controlling will keep people away. We can hide behind humour, and deflect from real conversations. We can live in the mind and intellectualise. We can avoid letting people give to us; being self-sufficient, always giving and never receiving.

Walls between us and God can contain anger or mistrust towards Him. They can be built from shame or a sense of unworthiness about ourselves. They can come from a damaged view of our self where we haven't received God's unconditional love, grace and forgiveness. Walls can grow from a belief that He doesn't care. They can stem from beliefs about God that are just not true. The Israelite slaves could easily have projected their experience of a cruel Pharaoh, who made their lives a misery, onto their view of God.

If we have gone through experiences where we couldn't cope with the difficult emotions, or they felt too shameful, walls can manifest as emotional disconnection, anaesthetising, retreating into the mind or intellectualising. In more extreme situations, we can disconnect from the experience and memories and separate from that part of ourselves.

Yet God in His wonderful love has a time and a place and a way for us to be healed and for those defences to come down.

In inner healing prayer sessions, I have seen so many special moments where these barriers have fallen away. As people have started to feel safe with God and able to trust Him, and as the lies they have been believing are exposed and truth received, the need for the walls disappears and the walls can come down. It is beautiful to see the peace that comes over people and see the tension and fear go.

The most important kind of wall is any wall between us and God. His unconditional love can't invade our souls when the walls are up. When we remove a few bricks, say of unbelief, and start to believe God might be there, we then see more light and develop some awareness of God. It's not until the wall comes right down between us that His love pours into us, saturates us and baptises us with His Spirit.

As I turned fourteen, I went to a Christian youth camp after a particularly difficult year at school. I was at a very low ebb and had arrived at the camp knowing no one. The next day I got chatting to a lovely girl who said she wanted to get filled with the Holy Spirit, and asked if I also wanted this. I had a strong reaction as if my whole being wanted that. I knew of the powerful experience at Pentecost where the disciples had been filled with the Holy Spirit and started speaking in tongues and were changed people from then on. I had known it was a very important thing to happen and I had prayed for it in the past, but then it was more from a place of knowing it was a good thing and that I wanted it. However, this time I knew I absolutely needed it. It was as if any wall between me and God completely came down and everything in me needed more. We went to find some leaders to pray with us. They started to pray and asked me if I wanted to receive a new measure of the Holy Spirit. As I heard their question I also saw, for the first time, a mini vision . . . of a narrow country footpath with high hedges and a gate to open. I knew this was an invitation to open the gate and travel that path . . . and that I had no idea what that meant. I looked in the vision for the alternative and I saw a motorway with many people along it. I thought back over the last few years at school and absolutely knew I needed a lot more, and I wanted a different route.

I had always believed in God and seen numerous answers to prayer. I had been blessed with parents who lived such an authentic faith and had taught me so much about God, the Bible and living God's way. I had not a shadow of a doubt of His existence and care for me, but this was a step further. It was choosing to open that little gate, travel that narrow path and surrender to whatever that meant. With a moment of 'Help! What does this mean?' the thought then came that 'God is love'[57] and I knew I had to be able to trust love. With elements of courage and trepidation, but also necessity, I said, 'Yes.' I was instantly overwhelmed by the presence and power of God. It was an indescribable feeling, tingly electric power and Presence around and within me and huge amounts of joy bubbling up from within . . . and the heavenly language of tongues just poured out of my mouth. We then experienced wave upon wave of joy and laughter for hours after. I can honestly say I have been different ever since, in a very good way.

There is an invitation of love, for the wall between us and God to come down. Father God is saying, 'You don't have to prove yourself, you don't have to hide, you don't need to be ashamed, and you don't need to be someone else. Just let My love in, let the walls come down. My love is true. I am love. It is not weakness to need Me. You were created to need Me, to live life with My Spirit inside you. Come to Me to be fully whole.'

---

57. 1 John 4:8.

The wall comes down.

Pause and encounter

Ask Father God:

Is it time for any wall I've created to come down?

Is there any wall between me and You?

Am I believing anything false about You or myself that has caused the wall?

I renounce the false belief that . . .

What is the truth?

Is there any wall I've built between myself and others?

Are there any false beliefs in the foundations of that wall?

I renounce the false belief that . . .

What is the truth?

Is there any offence or hurt I need to let go of and give to You and forgive?

I give you the pain of . . .and I choose to forgive . . .

Please help me take the wall down. I choose to look to You for my protection.

If you see a wall in your mind's eye, with Jesus' help, start taking it down.

Is there any defence or coping mechanism I no longer need that I can give to You?

I give my way of reacting by . . . to You . . . Please take it from me.

What do You give me in exchange?

Our Physical Body

On that day you will realise that I am in my Father,
and you are in me, and I am in you.

John 14:20

Jesus spoke to His disciples about this mind-blowing truth that not only is the Spirit of God in Jesus, but Jesus can also be in us and we can be in Jesus.

We have looked at how we can remove spiritual blockages to allow a far greater flow of God's Spirit into our spirit. We have looked at causes of those blockages, such as our walls of self-sufficiency, unbelief or perhaps anger towards God. There are also the spiritual blocks from involvement in the dark realm. As we unblock the footholds of the adversary and surrender ourselves to God's lordship, our spirit becomes alive with His Spirit and connects to the riches of heaven. We start to live in the reality of what Jesus said 'you are in me, and I am in you'.

We are holistic beings made of spirit, mind, emotions and body. Our spirit is the part of us that connects with God and can sense the spiritual realm. Not only does our spirit need the life-giving flow of the Spirit of God, but our mind and emotions also need this flow of life.

We have looked at the healing of our souls as we receive God's truth, shed old mindsets and release deep pain to God. God's Spirit refreshes our thinking and transforms our attitudes. As we open up our emotional life to God, the flow of His life-giving Spirit can release suppressed emotions, and bring balance and wholeness into that area too.

The flow of His life-giving love needs to continue into our physical bodies. Do I have blocks to this flow into my body? How connected am I to my body? How much do I understand what it is carrying? Do I love it? Do I cherish it?

We are probably very aware of physical aches and pains or fatigue, but maybe not so aware of the deeper things our body is carrying. Our body can carry fear as a result of trauma. It can have lost its peace and ability to truly rest. If we have pushed it too hard and not listened to it, it can be over-reliant on adrenaline to keep going. It can be carrying repressed emotions and stress.

Our bodies can also carry shame and feel dirty. I have seen beautiful moments in inner healing prayer sessions where people have released their shame to Jesus and asked Him to take if from them. They have felt themselves being washed clean. One person said it was as if their blood had been dark and all the darkness went.

Resentment can block the flow of life in any relationship. We see that in how we relate to God and to other people; resentment is a bottleneck on life-giving connection. I would suggest this also applies to our bodies. If we resent our body or resent how it is coping, we don't have a wholesome connection with it. Resentments, judgements, or rejection of our body will hinder the flow of His life to it.

If we cherish the body God gave us, we will listen to it; we will look after it well. We are created for a flow of the life of God through our spirit, into our mind and emotions, and into our body; and we need to keep the flow unhindered.

It may be important for us to forgive our body for letting us down, as we see it. We may need to ask our body and God to forgive us for not treating our body well, or resenting it, or not cherishing it. We may need to ask forgiveness for any way we have rejected it or disliked it. Then we can rebuild a loving embracing connection with our body. We can pray compassionately for it and not cause a block to the flow of God's power.

Pause and encounter

Ask Jesus:

Is my body carrying anything that You want to release it from?

Give the fear/shock/shame/. . . to Jesus and ask Him to cleanse you and carry it for you . . . ask Him to show you what He is doing.

(There may be a lot more to do in this area, revisiting memories with Jesus, finding false beliefs and truth, and forgiving . . .)

What do You give me in exchange?

Do I need to change any ways I have been viewing my body?

Am I believing anything false about my body?

And I reject the false belief that . . .

What is the truth – how do You see my body?

Is there any attitude or way that I have treated my body that I need to ask forgiveness for?

Jesus, please forgive me for . . .

Body, I am sorry for treating you in this way, please forgive me.

Jesus, is there any other way I have hindered the flow of Your blessing to my body?

Is there anything I need to do differently?

Jesus, I ask You to help me to love my body. Please bless my body with peace, healing and the flow of your power. I ask for Your help and wisdom in how to treat well the body You have given me, and to cherish it.

Grace

This journey is not a test of whether or not we will make it to the Promised Land. It is not about whether we passed or failed. We may have made many mistakes, failed many times, tripped and stumbled, and that is OK. This is a journey of growth and transformation; a journey of encountering God's grace, His compassion and forgiveness. For every time we trip and stumble and go astray, He is there to welcome us back; He is there to pick us up; He is there to cleanse us and heal our wounds.

Unless we have made mistakes and 'failed', we will never truly understand His grace. Unless we have struggled, we may self-righteously judge others, rather than have compassion. We may have sympathy, but we may not have true empathy. God uses our trips and stumbles for good.

King David's adultery with Bathsheba[58] is one of the great examples of God's grace. King David did reap consequences of his sin, with terrible guilt and shame, and the baby that had been conceived, died. Yet from his true remorse, David received absolute forgiveness. Out of God's incredible grace, God even then blessed the marriage to the extent that Jesus is a direct descendant of David and Bathsheba. There is nothing too big that cannot be completely forgiven by God's grace.

---

58. 2 Samuel 11.

The waterfall of Grace and Forgiveness to wash us clean.

Though your sins are like scarlet,
they shall be as white as snow . . .
Isaiah 1:18

The Encouragements

While the big prayers are, perhaps, not yet being answered, there may be many answers to little prayers; or just little things that God does along the way that show He cares. On one front, it may seem that nothing is shifting, that prayers are getting nowhere; but in another area of our life, God is blessing us. It is like His hugs for us. He is showing us that He is right there with us, walking through this valley with us. Let's keep an attitude of praise, of looking for those little signs of His love, those hugs. Let's hold on to an attitude of thankfulness that sees and receives. Let's walk through the valley knowing the love of the Father, thankful for all His little encouragements and hugs, simply trusting He is leading us up and out, to a better place.

If we keep our eyes on what God is doing, rather than what isn't happening, if we keep our eyes on His love for us and how He is demonstrating it, then He gives us grace to keep walking and to keep trusting. His love keeps us going.

A little hug that often happens for me is that I frequently look at the clock when it is fourteen minutes past the hour. This has happened so many times I know it's not a coincidence. One morning I was mulling over whether this was because I was just more aware when it was fourteen minutes past and not registering all the other times. I happened to look at the clock that morning four times and every single time it was fourteen minutes past a different hour. I had my answer. For me it's a special number; it's my birthday. I was born on the fourteenth day of the month. In the Bible, fourteen relates to the concept of double portion. (Seven is related to perfection and completion, which is a factor of fourteen.) This feels very relevant to coming out of the wilderness and illness season. God is showing me He's there, He loves me and He's absolutely in the centre of the timings of my life. He is giving me a hug.

Flowers of praise and thankfulness for the hugs.

Though the fig-tree does not bud
and there are no grapes on the vines,
though the olive crop fails
and the fields produce no food,
though there are no sheep in the sheepfold
and no cattle in the stalls,
yet I will rejoice in the LORD,
I will be joyful in God my Saviour.

Habakkuk 3:17-18

The Silence

In the story of the little Jewish boy in the concentration camp (*Life Is Beautiful*[59]), his time of hiding in the box was a time when his father left him and went in search of his wife. The time when Moses went up the mountain and received the Ten Commandments was a time when he left the Israelites behind. Sometimes there are times when it seems like Father God has gone, when there is silence, when our prayers seem to hit the ceiling and bounce back and we don't know why.

It's not necessarily that we have withdrawn from God, or that we have done anything wrong, or that something has come between us and God (but that can be the case). The silence can be a time of testing. Job, in the Old Testament, had an extended period before God answered and spoke to him. It's a time when our trust is put to the test.

In the film, the little boy steadfastly trusted and obeyed his father. He had implicit faith, trusting and believing in his father's love, to the extent that it saved his life. Yet when Moses left the Israelites to go up the mountain, most of them turned to other comforts. They reverted to their old idols and built a golden calf to worship.[60]

---

59. *Life Is Beautiful*, distributed by Cecchi Gori Group (Italy) and Miramax Films (USA/International).
60. Exodus 32.

The times of silence reveal our heart; it reveals where our trust lies. It's not a reflection of God's heart towards us. The absolute truth is that He has not left us; He has not abandoned us. The sun has gone behind the clouds for reasons we do not know and we may not understand for years, if at all in this lifetime. Let's not turn our backs on Him or turn to a 'golden calf' during this time.

The sun is still there; it has just been behind a cloud.

Pause and encounter

Ask Jesus:

Have I turned to any 'golden calf' instead of You?

If so, ask for forgiveness and try to make a choice to want to walk away from the 'golden calf', and ask for His wisdom and help in how to do so.

Am I believing anything false about Your presence with me?

I reject the false belief that . . .

(e.g. that You have abandoned me, that You're not there for me . . .)

What is the truth?

I receive the truth that . . .

Is there anyone I need to forgive who has helped me to believe this?

Is there anyone I need to forgive who has influenced me to turn to the 'golden calf'?

I choose to forgive . . . for their influence on me and the consequences this has had. I release them to You, Jesus, in forgiveness.

For a Greater Glory

The silence may now be over, but perhaps we are not seeing the answers we are looking for? We often hear it said that Jesus healed everyone who came to Him, but maybe we don't find that reality for ourselves.

Let's take the example of our lives being a metaphorical house and the house is cold. So, we come to Jesus asking for an electric heater, but He doesn't provide it. Jesus sees the house has windows that don't shut properly, letting in cold air, and this is because there is a crack in the foundations and mould in one of the walls. He knows the best answer isn't an electric heater but the whole house to be repaired and a new central heating system installed.

Jesus does still heal everyone who comes to Him, but the question is *what* is He wanting to heal today? For the non-believer or new believer, He wants to heal unbelief and reveal His love, and often this is seen through powerful answers to prayer and physical healing. For those further down the road, His first priority is usually to do the bigger healing work and heal the root causes and entry points of what is 'damaged'.

When Jesus doesn't answer our prayers immediately or in the way we want them to be answered, we must know that He has greater plans. His love is taking us on a different route to a profound answer to our deepest needs. His love for the world at large is taking us on a route of transformation for a far greater display of His glory.

> 'For my thoughts are not your thoughts,
> neither are your ways my ways,' declares the LORD.
>
> *Isaiah 55:8*

Mary, Martha and Lazarus were devoted followers of Jesus. Mary particularly loved to sit at Jesus' feet and learn and absorb and feed on everything He taught. Then Lazarus, Mary's brother, got dangerously ill.[61] They sent for Jesus to come and pray for Lazarus. Mary absolutely knew that if Jesus came, Lazarus would be well. Yet Jesus purposely delayed in coming. He knew He had to wait. When He arrived He found them in mourning, as Lazarus had died. Jesus was greatly moved, and wept. Mary didn't go out to meet Him on arrival. When Jesus came to her, Mary in her grief poured out her distress to Him. Why had He delayed His coming, when He could have healed Lazarus if He'd come straight away?

I wonder if things died in Mary when Lazarus died. Did some trust in Jesus die? Did faith in His nature of love and compassion get broken? Did a belief that God is always good get fractured?

I wonder what went on in Jesus? He knew He had done the right thing, that He had obeyed the Father. Yet He felt the grief and depths of anguish which He could have prevented. Yet He

---

61.   Read the story of Lazarus in John 11.

also saw more. He saw the bigger picture and He knew what was coming.

After Lazarus had been dead for four days, Jesus prayed and commanded him back to life. Lazarus hobbled out of the tomb bound in his grave clothes. They unwrapped the linen and he walked free, alive and well. Many came to believe in Jesus after this miracle. It was as Jesus had said 'if you believe, you will see the glory of God'.[62]

I wonder what then also was resurrected in Mary? Did her trust in Jesus go to a completely new level? Was her faith in God's love and power established on a new plane?

So often we just don't understand what is going on, and we can't. We don't see the bigger picture. We don't see God's plans for the greater glory He is going to reveal. In our misunderstanding, we lash out at God, or we withdraw, or walls go up in our hearts. We don't see that God is greatly moved by our suffering, that He too feels the pain. He longs for us to trust in His goodness and in His love, even though we don't understand. He is saying to us too, 'if you believe, you will see the glory of God'.

Let's be real like Mary and pour out our distress to God; let's be honest with Him, but also let's hear what He has to say. Let's know that He is closer than we can imagine and that He feels our pain too. Though we don't understand, and we may have to let go of understanding for the present, let's hold on to the truth that God is good. Even when evidence seems to point to the contrary, God is good, 'God is love'; in God 'there is no darkness'.

---

62. John 11:40.

If you believe, you will see the glory of God.

God is light; in Him there is no darkness at all
1 John 1:5

Whoever does not love does not know God,
because God is love.
1 John 4:8

Pause and encounter

If this has touched you, maybe spend some time with Jesus expressing how you're really feeling.

See if you can let go of the need to understand, and give that to God.

See if you can let go of any anger or bitterness you may be holding towards Him, and ask Him to take it and forgive.

Ask forgiveness for where you have judged God without knowing the bigger picture, without knowing the glory to come.

Give Him your heart with all the disappointment, grief and pain. Ask Him for His healing.

Give Him the broken trust, the doubts about His goodness and any unbelief. Ask Him to restore your faith in His love and goodness.

Faith

The death of Lazarus must have been an enormous test of Mary's view of Jesus. The blows of adversity or the 'wilderness' journey can shake our faith. When it really hurts, or when it doesn't make sense, it can challenge our faith in God, in prayer, or in His goodness.

Of the twelve spies who went ahead to explore the Promised Land, only Joshua and Caleb saw it through eyes of faith. They saw its abundance and saw that it was good. The rest reacted in fear at the size of the people there. Their report caused fear amongst the Israelites, who then grumbled against God, complaining that He had brought them out of Egypt to destroy them. The ongoing stubbornness, grumbling and rebellion greatly displeased God and He delayed the entry into the Promised Land by forty years. Joshua and Caleb were the only ones who had come out of Egypt who were allowed to leave the wilderness and live in the Promised Land.[63]

Another group who never entered the Promised Land were the tribes of Reuben and Gad. When the forty years were up, these two tribes chose to settle on the east side of the Jordan

---

63.   Numbers 13:17 – 14:3; Numbers 14:26-35; Numbers 26:65.

River.[64] They didn't want to go into the Promised Land. They had become comfortable with where they were.

Faith, by its very definition, is holding on to what we do not yet see.[65] Significantly, God wanted the Israelites to keep recounting and remembering all His miracles and past provision. The Passover festival was instituted to remember how God delivered them from slavery. When it's not making sense for us now, it is so helpful to hold on to all the times that God has helped us in the past. Remembering God's faithfulness in the past helps anchor our faith when we are shaken; remembering all the answers to prayer, all the many 'coincidences' that were so clearly orchestrated by God. God doesn't change;[66] if He was good then, He is still good now. His promises in the Bible still hold.

When I was young, I had such a simple and easy faith in God. I saw so many answers to prayer that it didn't even cross my mind to question God's love and faithfulness. If it was raining right up to the point of my birthday party, I had prayed, so I knew the rain would stop the moment the party started and it always did. It didn't occur to me to doubt that it would. Maybe that's why Jesus said, 'Truly I tell you, unless you change and become like little children, you will never enter the kingdom of heaven.'[67] Childlike faith is still the type of faith that God wants us to have. When God said, 'Never will I leave you; never will I forsake you',[68] He meant it.

Faith starts with the bedrock that God is good; He is always good. Faith stands on the promise that 'in all things God works

---

64. Numbers 32:1-5.
65. Hebrews 11:1.
66. Malachi 3:6.
67. Matthew 18:3.
68. Hebrews 13:5; see also Deuteronomy 31:6.

for the good of those who love him, who have been called according to his purpose'.[69] Jesus asked the question 'Which of you, if your son asks for bread, will give him a stone?' He went on to say, 'how much more will your Father in heaven give good gifts to those who ask him!'[70] Wherever the winds of adversity may blow, God is good . . . always good. God loves us . . . always loves us.

Although robbery and destruction are from the adversary, it seems that God does sometimes allow us some 'battle experience' for our own good, to strengthen us and stretch us further. He doesn't want us defeated by these battles; He wants us to overcome and win. As we see the victories, our faith grows.

Holding in faith what we don't yet clearly see, through the mist.

69. Romans 8:28.
70. Matthew 7:9-11.

Adversity can act like a refining fire. It separates what was just a mental assent to faith in God, from what is true faith in our hearts. We can have just been believing what we have been told, but not have really known it in our hearts. The shaking is a refining process that reveals the true faith.

> In all this you greatly rejoice, though now for a little while you may have had to suffer grief in all kinds of trials.
> These have come so that the proven genuineness of your faith
> – of greater worth than gold, which perishes even though refined by fire
> – may result in praise, glory and honour when Jesus Christ is revealed.
>
> *1 Peter 1:6-7*

Paul said, 'I pray that the eyes of your heart may be enlightened'.[71] We can hear over and over again that God loves us. Then one day we really 'hear' it; that God loves me, the vulnerable me, warts and all; He loves *me*. We hear the truth in our hearts; it has landed, and we are changed.

Walking through adversity we find that optimism is not enough. As it runs out, we need to find true faith.

---

71. Ephesians 1:18.

The heart enlightened with faith from God.

The disciples said to Jesus, 'Increase our faith!'[72] It is interesting how Jesus responded. He didn't pray for them or give more evidence of His power. Instead He said, 'If you have faith as small as a mustard seed' – that is, even if it's extremely small – 'you can say to this mulberry tree' (i.e. the problem), '"Be uprooted and planted in the sea," and it will obey you.'[73] He is saying, use the little faith you do have and pray, speak to the problem with the authority I have given you in My name, and you will see results. That is how your faith will grow.

We may not have faith for big things yet, but if we start with praying about the little things, we will see God's faithfulness there, and faith will grow. We should never think we mustn't bother God about little things. He loves to be involved in the detail, in the small things, as He wants us to know that He

72.   Luke 17:5
73.   Luke 17:6.

hears and He loves and He cares about every detail of our lives. Seeing His answers in these smaller areas is exactly how our faith can grow.

Faith comes from true 'hearing';[74] when the Holy Spirit reveals God's truth to us and opens the eyes of our heart. Faith grows as a gift from God. It also comes from acting on the little faith we do have, from praying and speaking with Jesus' authority to the problems, and seeing God move. It comes, too, from removing blocks to faith.

Faith is key to believing that what God has promised will happen. It is key to trusting that 'God is love'.[75] Faith is key in how we pray. Faith is key in warding off discouragement, like a shield against the darts that try to pierce us. Faith doesn't see us as stuck in the desert or stuck in prison. Faith knows that we are just passing through. We are rising up. We are on our way to a much better place.

74. Romans 10:17.
75. 1 John 4:8.

Holding the shield of faith

Contending

After the Israelites had lived in the Promised Land for generations, and after very many warnings from God about disobedience and following other gods, they were invaded and taken captive by the Babylonians. They lived as captives in Babylon for decades. Daniel was an Israelite prophet in Babylon at the end of this period. From his studying of Jeremiah's prophecies, he saw that their captivity should come to an end after seventy years.[76] So he took it upon himself to contend in prayer for their deliverance and the ending of their captivity. He didn't expect it to just happen; he knew the Israelites had their part to play; they had to be obedient to God's commands in order to receive God's blessings. He poured himself out in prayer in repentance for their disobedience and asking for forgiveness. With prayer and fasting, he pleaded with God to forgive, to hear and to act.

There was a powerful conflict in the heavenly realm to bring the captivity to an end. After some time, an angel came to Daniel and told him his prayers were heard as soon as he started praying, but the angel was held up for twenty-one days battling with evil powers.[77] So there is sometimes a struggle in the

---

76. Daniel 9:2.
77. Daniel 10:12-13.

heavenly realm for our prayers to be answered. At times, we may need to persevere in prayer, pursuing God's power to break through in our situations.

Coming back to our story of the journey to the Promised Land, when the Israelites finally crossed the river Jordan and entered the Promised Land, they immediately came against the fortified city of Jericho. An angel of God met with Joshua and told him that God was giving them the city.[78]

They had to walk round the walls of Jericho for six days carrying the Ark of the Covenant, with seven priests blowing trumpets and then walk round seven times on the seventh day – and then the walls fell down![79] There are some significant points to take from this incident on the principles of winning battles and contending in prayer.

Previously there were times when God had told Moses to skirt around some enemy territories, as He wasn't giving them into their hands.[80] Here God clearly said it was His will for them to conquer Jericho. They didn't approach the city in their own wisdom, in their own strength, or with their own battle strategies. They carried the Ark of the Covenant, which represents carrying the Presence of God. Blowing trumpets (or rams' horns), is a call to advance, a call to battle and a fearless announcement of their arrival. There was a perseverance in repeatedly circling the city until the walls fell.

As we contend in prayer for walls to come down, we first need to be sure this is a 'city' God has given us. When Jesus speaks of prayer, He so often qualifies His promises of answering with

78. Joshua 5:14 – 6:5.
79. Joshua 6.
80. Deuteronomy 2:9.

'[if you] ask in my name'.[81] His 'name' refers to His nature, who He is, His Spirit. Jesus is saying we need to be praying in line with His Spirit and His will.

They carried the Ark of the Covenant with them. When contending in prayer, we so need to pray from a place of first drawing close to God. This helps us move away from praying with just the mind to praying in the flow of the Holy Spirit.

I have found, when praying, if I tune into my spirit and see if I have a sense of assurance, as if there is a green light, then I really pray into the issue. If I don't get the green light, then I try to sense what I should be praying instead, tuning into God's agenda and will. As we grow in this way of praying, we are increasingly praying 'in the Spirit',[82] a more powerful, Spirit-led way.

Praying 'in the Spirit' also includes praying in tongues;[83] a powerful gift to ask for. When we pray in tongues, we are praying in line with God's will, without knowing exactly what we are praying. We can bring a person before God in our hearts, then pray in tongues for them. The Holy Spirit is praying through us for what is really needed.

However, sometimes when praying, I will sense a block; there may be something to ask forgiveness for, and God will show me what that is. Then that block or heaviness will lift and there will be a greater ease in prayer and the sense of His presence. Sometimes we need to reject unbelief or not having our faith and reliance fully on God.

---

81. John 14:13.
82. Ephesians 6:18.
83. 1 Corinthians 12:10.

Praying with a 'blowing trumpets' mentality is not praying from a place of defeat, or weariness, or unbelief, but from a place of authority, from knowing God has given this into our hands.

As we pray in line with the Holy Spirit, each time we pray, the foundations of the 'wall' are shaken. The more we pray, the more the 'wall' will crumble and eventually fall.

Walking through prolonged adversity or a wilderness experience can challenge our passion and perseverance to pray for our situation. Maybe God wants to grow in *how* we pray. We also need to be on guard for all those distractions that try to deflect us from praying. It is no coincidence that almost anything else can seem appealing or important to do right now, when we need to pray. Truly grasping the power of prayer is essential.

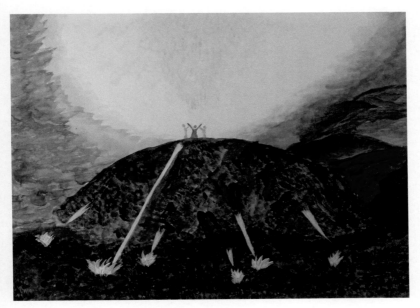

Contending in prayer.

The Promised Land

So what does the Promised Land represent?

Interestingly, the Promised Land was the *original* homeland of the Israelites. It was the place that God had called Abraham to settle in – Canaan, now Israel, the birthplace of the Israelite nation. When famine came to the region, they followed Joseph to Egypt where there was food, and remained there for 430 years.[84] When they grew in numbers and became prosperous, the Egyptians turned against them and made them slaves. So journeying to the Promised Land was coming home.

Perhaps the Promised Land also partly represents who we were born to be, our original homeland, the real people with our full potential. Healed people who have been made whole. Liberated people who are no longer slaves to wrong powers; the people God had originally planned, living in our calling and gifting.

There is a sense of coming home; coming home to our true selves. But wider than that, there is a coming home to God's heart. The barriers between us and God have come down. The walls of shame and unworthiness have been removed. The orphan slaves have discovered their loving Father and have come home. They have come home to where they truly belong.

---

84.   Exodus 12:40-41.

The Bible often refers to *inheriting* the Promised Land.[85] So it also relates to our inheritance from God; what He wants to impart to us. God has a great deal that He wants to give us, inwardly and outwardly. He wants to pervade us with peace, inner joy and a security in His love. He also has a destiny and calling on our lives that can bring a very real sense of fulfilment. He wants to fill us to overflowing with His Holy Spirit, so that we really do walk through life empowered and guided by Him. He wants to provide that extra factor, that 'anointing' to the activities He has called us to, so there is an injection of something that is more than ourselves; an added charge of power, insight, wisdom and love. He wants to give us His heart for people; a heart for the unlovely and the broken. He wants to give us access to heaven's resources.

The Promised Land is a place of fruitfulness. The descriptions of this land are full of the abundance of its fruit and produce. God works through us to bring His life, truth, healing and wholeness to others, as an overflow of our life. Our lives bear fruit. We may be unaware of this overflow, but wherever the Holy Spirit has brought transformation in us, there is a natural impact on the lives of others. Our lives begin to display the fruit of the Holy Spirit spoken of by Paul: 'love, joy, peace, patience, kindness, goodness, faithfulness, gentleness, self-control'.[86]

---

85.   Numbers 34:2.
86.   Galatians 5:22-23, NASB.

Fruitfulness and abundance in the Promised Land.

The Promised Land is very different from the wilderness. Far from being a stripped down, harsh place, it is rich and abundant. It is a foretaste of a far, far greater freedom, restoration, healing, abundance and joy in the life to come. We hopefully enter and experience much of it in this life, but there will be much, much more to come in our eternal home.

Through the wilderness experience, we have been truly humbled. We have needed God at a whole new level. We have been emptied of ourselves to leave so much more space for God. So when we start to see fruitfulness and harvest, we know this is not of ourselves. This is for God's glory. I remember seeing some exquisite, dazzling blossom in a hedgerow, lit up by the sun's rays. It really was quite special and I was drawn to it; I wanted to have a closer look. Looking round the back of the shrub where the sun wasn't shining on it, it was an especially drab, dull blossom . . . the glory goes to God.

A cracked clay pot, that God's light can shine through.

The Promised Land is not heaven, because it still has challenges. The Israelites did not 'inherit' the whole land overnight. They had to destroy the places where previous tribes had worshipped other gods, known in the Bible as 'high places.'[87] If not removed, these 'high places' would cause the Israelites many problems. These were strongholds of evil power they had to pull down. They had further adversaries to defeat as they claimed the land bit by bit. We also will have an ongoing process of growing into everything God has for us and defeating the strongholds (or destroying the high places) in our lives.

There was a phase of conquering the Promised Land before they settled down to live in it. When the Israelites came to the Promised Land, they found other enemy tribes who lived there. Chapters 2 and 3 of Judges state that God left other tribes in the land and He didn't drive them out straight away. He did this, we read,[88] to teach warfare to the young Israelites who had had no battle experience. Let's see this as symbolic of spiritual truth. God knows we need 'battle experience' to become those who are equipped and practised at closing the door to the entry points of the evil one; experienced at reclaiming territory in our lives from oppressive occupation.

Through 'battle experience' we learn to follow God's ways of rescuing situations, which are far better than our ways. This is part of *Promised Land living*, being skilled warriors who reclaim occupied territory, drive out the oppressor and bring light into the darkness.

---

87. Numbers 33:52.
88. Judges 3:1.

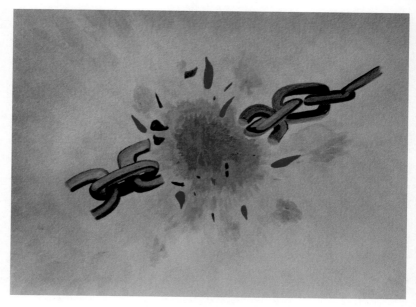

Breaking chains of oppression.

The wilderness journey has brought things to the surface in our life to be cleansed and healed. It has taught us to flow with the Holy Spirit and live out of a place of dependency and obedience to God. Then the battles to conquer the Promised Land equip us further.

God wants people He can trust; people who face their battles His way; who don't try to fix things in their own strength, but lean on His wisdom and direction. The way the Israelites won their battles as they entered the Promised Land showed they had learnt to walk in obedience. The defeat of Jericho, by walking round it blowing trumpets, showed they were listening and obeying, and they were victorious. If God can trust us, He can give us more.

In Ephesians, Paul says we are 'seated . . . in the heavenly places',[89] which is a huge concept. He is saying this is the truth regarding where God has placed us when He saved us by His grace. We have an invitation to walk into the reality of this. There is a parallel with the *process* of shedding the 'slave' identity'; similarly, we grow into and awaken to our dwelling place of being 'seated . . . in the heavenly places'.

'Heavenly places' are our new home, our new citizenship, our source of authority in prayer, the place we need to start the day from. It means we have access to heaven's resources, to bring heaven's power and joy to earth. Promised Land living is living from this position, and with the identity that goes with being an inhabitant of 'heavenly places'.

Seated in the heavenly places.

89. Ephesians 2:6, NASB.

> and [God] raised us up with Him, and seated us
> with Him in the heavenly places in Christ Jesus . . .
>
> *Ephesians 2:6, NASB*

Promised Land living is no longer about *us*. We have moved into a dependency on God like never before. It is the life-giving way to come though the wilderness and out the other side transformed. Jesus said the Son (that is Himself) 'can do nothing of Himself, unless it is something He sees the Father doing'.[90] We are being drawn and called into living more like Jesus, where we are in tune and connected with the Holy Spirit. It is like we are in the flow of the river of the Spirit; flowing with His plans and thoughts and ways.

As we journey into the Promised Land, and work through areas of struggle and genuinely break free of strongholds in our lives, we gain spiritual authority in those very areas. We gain strength, understanding, wisdom, insight and real ability to help others walk free. We have a level of authority in prayer for other people in these areas; a new level of power in prayer.

We are also more easily aware of those same struggles in others and have the non-judgemental true empathy and compassion to walk alongside. We have been equipped and our hearts have been opened to others to a new degree.

I was at a training course once where we were encouraged to go and pray for people we felt drawn to pray for, and pray freedom over them for the issue that had been the biggest

---

90. John 5:19, NASB.

struggle we had overcome in our own lives. A person in the room seemed highlighted to me so I just prayed a simple prayer of commanding the same issue off their life, in Jesus' name, and praying for them to be free. It was that simple. But it had come from a long struggle of breaking free in that area in my own life. Power from the Holy Spirit came on them. They fell down back into their seat, looking stunned, with the Holy Spirit clearly ministering to them. Later the person said it felt as if power had gone right through them. This doesn't happen every time I pray for people! There is more – far more – than we realise.

Pause and encounter

Ask Jesus:

How am I viewing my identity?

Am I believing anything that is not true that is preventing me from knowing that I am seated in 'heavenly places'?

I reject the belief that ...

What is the truth?

I receive the truth that ...

What do You want to say about my identity?

A harvest is coming.

In the Old Testament, quite frequently after winning battles against other tribes, the Israelites took *plunder* from their enemies. With God, we don't come out of our battle experiences just scarred, wounded and broken. Our healing and restoration, with God's tender healing power, may take a time, but then we can walk away healed, strengthened and with *plunder*. We walk forward with powerful prayer and an ability, working with the Holy Spirit, to help others walk free in the very areas where we have overcome.

The Spirit of the Sovereign LORD is on me,
because the LORD has anointed me
to proclaim good news to the poor.
He has sent me to bind up the broken-hearted,
to proclaim freedom for the captives
and release from darkness for the prisoners ...

Instead of your shame
you will receive a double portion,
and instead of disgrace
you will rejoice in your inheritance.
And so you will inherit a double portion in your land,
and everlasting joy will be yours.

Isaiah 61:1,7

Leaving the Wilderness

The transition to the Promised Land also means leaving the wilderness behind. There may be things we need to leave behind, perhaps regret, anger, self-pity or disappointment over the losses or struggles of the past. We need to really let these go, or else we will continue to live with these chains holding us back.

When Lazarus came back to life, after Jesus prayed, he had to come out of the tomb, and the grave clothes had to go.[91]

We are not the person we were. We are not defined by our mistakes, losses, or struggles. We have been raised up, changed and healed. God makes all things new. We have a new season ahead to embrace.

---

91. See John 11:1-44.

Wonder, at the unfolding of what is fresh and new.

Pause and encounter

Ask Jesus:

Is there anything of the past I need to let go of?

Is there an old identity I need to let go of?

. . . spend some time giving these to Jesus and asking what He wants to gives in exchange.

Forget the former things;
do not dwell on the past.

See, I am doing a new thing!
Now it springs up; do you not perceive it?

Isaiah 43:18-19

The Treasures of the Deep

God once gave me a moving image whilst praying, of a pile of clothes on the ground. I knew each item represented a difficult, painful or challenging experience I'd walked through. I saw Jesus go to each item of clothing, search through the pockets, and in each pocket there was a piece of gold. He put those pieces of gold into a treasure chest, and I had a treasure chest full of gold.

Treasures acquired from overcoming the challenges.

Another picture He gave me was of a long-distance walker returning from travels to far-flung places across deserts and foreign terrains. The person was lean, fit, in serious need of a bath, weathered and strengthened by the journey, and glad to be at the end of it! She had a satchel over her shoulder, which was full of jewels and exotic spices collected from her travels.

Lean and fit from the journey.

Yet, there was a chasm of pain between her and Father God waiting at the end of her journey. The arduous demands of the journey had – perhaps inevitably – caused some deep wounds. She had to encounter Jesus in the chasm of pain; to release the pain to Him and receive His healing touch and truth. This brought healing to the wounds and closed the chasm. She could then fully end her desert journey in the embrace of the Father.

When I painted this picture, I painted the fit athlete walking through the desert with the bag of treasures and spices. This person was in good shape. She was the inner person, the spirit person. Yet, when I painted the picture of the girl standing beside the chasm looking across at Father God, that person turned out to be thin, pale and in ragged clothes. She was the outer person, the body that had borne the brunt of the storm and had been battered relentlessly. There lies the key difference; the outward person may be afflicted, weary and bruised, but the inner person has been strengthened, transformed and has collected treasures along the way.

Much Afraid, from the allegory *Hinds' Feet on High Places*, had to put a pebble in her bag each time she had to lay something down on an altar, or each time she learned a new truth. When she reached the end of her journey up the mountain, she found that her bag no longer contained ugly pebbles, but dazzling jewels. The Shepherd then embedded them in a golden crown for her to wear.

She had gathered the 'treasures of the deep' along the way.

> Therefore, we do not lose heart.
> Though outwardly we are wasting away,
> yet inwardly we are being renewed day by day.
>
> For our light and momentary troubles are achieving for us an eternal glory that far outweighs them all.
>
> *2 Corinthians 4:16-17*

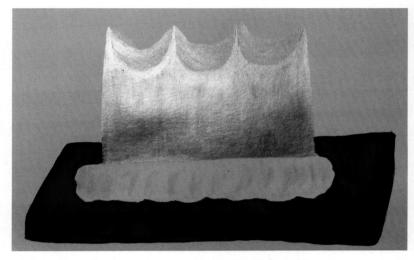

'Blessed is the one who perseveres under trial because, having stood the test, that person will receive the crown of life that the Lord has promised to those who love him.' James 1:12

In Matthew 13, Jesus tells a parable of a pearl of great value that has been found in a field. Due to its incredible value and worth, the person who discovers it sells everything they have in order to buy that field. Perhaps the desert is a place of discovering more of the incredible worth of that pearl of great value.

When we are struggling with loss or laying down desires on the altar, it often doesn't seem that we are exchanging them for something so much greater – the 'pearl of great value';[92] it just seems it's too hard. We can't see the true worth of the 'pearl of great value', as we are blinded by the pain, or we have yet to experience the pearl's value. Yet when we find those hard pebbles transformed into jewels, when we find that we have

---

92.   Matthew 13:45-46, NASB.

walked into the Father's embrace, when we find the 'treasures of the deep', we know that somehow it was worth it, that we truly have found the 'pearl of great value'.

> Afflicted city, lashed by storms and not comforted,
> I will rebuild you with stones of turquoise,
> your foundations with lapis lazuli.
>
> I will make your battlements of rubies,
> your gates of sparkling jewels,
> and all your walls of precious stones.
>
> *Isaiah 54:11-12*
>
> You will be a crown of splendour in the LORD's hand,
> a royal diadem in the hand of your God.
>
> *Isaiah 62:3*

Crossing the Jordan

In due season, the desert journey will end with reaching the river Jordan and arrival in the Promised Land. The prison doors open and the captive is set free. The dawn breaks and the night is over. The winter ends and spring has come.

It was very likely that the Israelites crossed into the Promised Land close to the place that Jesus was baptised by John the Baptist. Baptism represents a burial of the old life and a rising up into a new life with God.[93] As we cross the river Jordan at this baptismal site, there is a deeper fulfilment of the promise of rising up into the new life of resurrection living, full of the Holy Spirit and flowing with the Holy Spirit.

We walk forward into the new season, changed, equipped and empowered. We are leaning on Jesus and more in step with Him. We are following the Shepherd, hearing and knowing His voice more. We walk forward with deeper healing, standing taller, not bowed down but free. We move into more of our destiny, a new fulfilment and greater purpose. We find a richer level of fruitfulness from our lives.

---

93. Romans 6:4.

We have seen God's faithfulness and grown in faith and trust. The riches of solitude in the Father's love have borne fruit; we know the love of our Father in a far more real, life-changing way. We are ready to emerge from the solitude, from the chrysalis, and to embrace Promised Land living, released and free.

A wounded eagle that had been taken to a recovery centre,
is now released back into the wild,
healed and ready to fly again.

Liberty! Released and free.

We walk forward, living with a truer sense of our identity in God, of being 'seated . . . in the heavenly places'.[94] We are living more from where we belong. In our hearts, we have a deeper awareness of being beloved children of our heavenly Father. We are experiencing greater power of the Holy Spirit, praying with an increased degree of His authority and anointing, and seeing more of His power at work in and through our lives.

A new season has begun.

> My beloved spoke, and said to me:
> 'Rise up, my love, my fair one,
> And come away.
> For lo, the winter is past,
> The rain is over and gone.
> The flowers appear on the earth;
> The time of singing has come,
> And the voice of the turtledove
> Is heard in our land.
> *Song of Songs 2:10-12, NKJV*

---

94. Ephesians 2:6, NASB.

176

*Wearing new robes, transformed
and holding His sceptre of authority.*

And we all, who with unveiled faces contemplate
the LORD's glory, are being transformed into his
image with ever-increasing glory, which comes
from the LORD, who is the Spirit.

2 Corinthians 3:18

As a final note to end this part of the book, I love the inspiring true story of the horse Seabiscuit[95] during the Great Depression in the United States. He was a racehorse with so much potential, but he had been treated in a way that had significantly damaged him. He was broken in spirit. Yet an insightful trainer saw true value in him that no one else had seen; he saw a streak of a champion.

The trainer gradually rebuilt Seabiscuit's trust and unknotted his dysfunctional reactions. He encouraged and built the horse up to truly get into his stride and realise his exceptional potential. It was a long journey of healing and transformation. A journey with body-blow setbacks. They persevered, holding on with tenacious hope and keeping going when most would have given up.

Then came that wonderful day when, having recovered from a serious injury caused by an opponent who had tried to take him out, he won the top race in the United States . . . and gave hope and joy to a whole nation.

A beautiful illustration of how God, like the trainer, with His passionate love for us, sees the beauty and true potential in each of us. If we let Him, He can turn around the rough things we go through to get us on our feet again and bring us genuine healing and transformation. We are back on our feet, running that race[96] as the people we were always created to be; bringing His hope and joy to those around us; helping bring heaven to earth.

---

95.   Laura Hillenbrand, *Seabiscuit* (New York: Random House, 2001).
96.   I Corinthians 9:24.

The desert season is over!

Part 2

My Story

As I step back from the many years of illness, and ponder and reflect, I see many facets. I have felt God showing a parallel with the process of creating diamonds. Along with the pressure and heat to transform graphite into the totally new internal structure of a diamond, is the hewing process to create the faceted gem with many sparkling faces. It has been years of pressure and heat and chiselling and shaping. Though we see ourselves as the rough lumps of graphite, God sees us as diamonds in the making.

One of the first areas to receive the sharp cut in the refining process was my level of trusting God. After a year and half of largely being on sick pay and then gradually doing some part-time work, I knew that stirring in my heart that God was calling me to leave my job. Rationally I could see it didn't look likely that I would be well enough to do my job adequately for a very long time. There was too much pressure with it; many others relied on me for their work, it was not suited to part-time hours or working from home. However, my employer's sick pay was good, and where would it leave me financially if I left? It could be a very long time before I could handle a job like that again (and it was).

Then my employer announced a round of voluntary redundancies. I knew I had to have the courage to request it. They immediately rejected my application. But over the next few weeks I kept getting the phrase 'Let my people go' going round in my head. I knew God wanted me to leave, as much as that was a scary option. I had for years had a deep trust in God and seen His faithfulness over and over again, but this required another level of trust. It was a deep inner gulp moment and a big step of courage. So I started to pray they would let me go with the redundancy package. 'Let my people go' was the phrase relating to God wanting the Israelite slaves released from their slavery under Pharaoh in Egypt.[97] They eventually were released, taking with them wealth from the Egyptians as part of their leaving package.[98] About six weeks later, the day before those chosen for redundancy were to leave, I received a phone call to the effect that one person had pulled out of the redundancy programme, and if I could get forms signed by a solicitor that day, I could have the package and go tomorrow. It turned out that I received a maximum pay out. They included my seven-month sabbatical in the calculation and my many months of sick leave. With tax relief on the pay out, it lasted me at least two years. God was showing His faithfulness.

It seemed like my career was over and I had no idea of how this would work out. So I made a very clear pact with God. I said, 'You order my days.' Essentially, 'My time is Yours, You show the way, I trust You with taking me forward in this.' I have to say He has been phenomenally faithful in this. Over time, I gradually took on tutoring from home. My number of pupils built up exactly in line with my health and energy levels. Every time I wasn't well enough, my pupils all happened to cancel their

---

97. See for example Exodus 5:1.
98. Exodus 12:35-36.

lessons. This happened over and over again. It was the kindness of a very loving God.

Apart from a couple of tutoring adverts, all my work has come my way without me trying. One summer I felt quite prompted to contact a friend in Sweden. I had that inner assurance to go and visit. I wasn't sure why, but knew that I needed to go. Because of that visit, I acquired a perfect work contract with her husband. He needed to subcontract an area of work that was exactly my skill set. Over the years, other tailor-made for me, part-time contracts also came exactly at the right time, from other 'chance' meetings with people. One work contract ended exactly the day before inner healing prayer ministry training started up in my church. If ever I have found myself in my element, in what I am made for, it is in that realm.

In the first year or two of the illness, it was as if every area of strength I had was stripped away. It was years and years before I could cope with any pressure on me, or any level of stress. It was many months before the brain fog lifted and I could start thinking more clearly. The verse 'My grace is sufficient for you, for my power is made perfect in weakness'[99] took on a new level of meaning. That is to say, God's strength in us and for us is seen and experienced far more when we are 'weak'.

I remember one holiday, when I was at a particularly low ebb with my health, being taken on a trip to a beach where I really struggled to walk down to the sand. I picked up a shell, which I have kept ever since. I knew I had to always remember being so weak. Wherever I would come to later, whatever experiences I would move into, I needed always to know how weak I had been. Life had to be built on a bedrock of deep humility and

---

99. 2 Corinthians 12:9.

leaning on God. I would always need to know that it is by God's grace that I am where I am today.

Alongside knowing real weakness and vulnerability in my health is the experience of being sustained by God's grace. I truly feel that I have been carried through the illness. It could have been so much worse. I know many people who have had a much worse time with similar diagnoses. God's grace enabled me to cope and in some ways even thrive. I had to be very careful on where I focused. If I looked at everything that I was missing out on, or how rough it was, or if I entertained any self-pity, then I lost the grace to be at peace with my situation and I would go down. I kept afloat and even had joy and fulfilment if I stayed focused on where God was at work, where the good things were happening, where I could help others, on what I could learn, and if I held on to truth. Even though I was very restricted in what I could do, the things I could be involved in often had a quality about them. God was keeping me on a very short leash, but providing quality experiences and times with people.

Gradually over time, my health began to improve and medical treatments for Lyme disease, other infections and food intolerances were helping. I had more energy, but not much. It became very clear that in order to avoid cancelling almost every commitment I made, I had to check with the Holy Spirit before making any plans. If I did that, if I only said yes to things I had peace about and an assurance in my spirit, that 'yes, this was from God', then I would be well enough and I wouldn't need to cancel it. This became an overriding experience with God — learning to be led by His Spirit in how I spent my time, and not just for whilst I was ill; this was to be an ongoing way to live.

Learning to be led by the Holy Spirit in what I did was not a new theme to me. I had explored and experimented in that area very much, particularly in my early twenties. It came to me then that I needed to be led in how I *prayed*. So I stepped right back from praying whatever was in my mind. I tried to tune into that sense in my spirit of a resonance and sense of rightness, of assurance, when I was praying in line with God's will. When we flow with the Holy Spirit whilst praying, it leads to more powerful answers to prayer. It greatly reduces the disappointments from where we just aren't praying in line with God's will for today. It leads to being in tune, to praying where it really matters, to where God is at work.

One incident stands out on a day I was struggling with being ill and begging prayers were getting nowhere. A thought came to me, 'Is there anyone else I can encourage today?' A particular individual came to mind and then a verse from the Bible did as well. I emailed them with the comment, 'Just in case this is relevant or of help, this verse came to mind for you . . .' It turned out to be spot on and a very grateful email came back. I became more and more aware of when people were on my heart, not to ignore the thoughts, but to take note and act. There have been many times when feeling pretty rough myself, I have felt prompted to contact others to encourage them with something from God or in some other way, or pray for them. Over and over again it has been perfect timing or significant for them. It has been key for me to take my eyes off the illness, and absolutely banish any 'victim mentality'. Many of the pictures in this book have been painted whilst not feeling well. It has been so significant for me that those days weren't wasted, that value can still come out of the difficult times.

I heard some advice from someone that really stayed with me. He was saying in those times when you are stuck, effectively when you are in the 'wilderness' or the 'prison', then prepare for what is next. Use the time well, prepare for what may lie ahead, when you may not have the time to spare. Invest well. This should not be from a place of driven-ness or not being able to be at rest, but rather a change of mindset about the wilderness. It is not wasted time. It can be an important time of investment and preparation. It is changing us, but we also need to use it well. Paul in the New Testament used his times in prison to write powerful letters that have been read by millions ever since. Again this needs to come from the Holy Spirit guiding us, otherwise we can drive ourselves and miss God's best for today.

The theme grew of 'don't let the desire to get well be your overriding priority'. Getting well was not to be the most important thing. The agenda had to become, 'What is God wanting to say to me today? What is He wanting to do in me or through me?' This day is for Him and His purposes. I remember an extremely timely opening of a book by Watchman Nee on a page where he was begging God to heal him and God clearly telling him to carry on doing what He had asked him to do; and that God would heal him along the way as he did so.

Learning to tune into His voice more and receiving more gifting in hearing Him has been another key facet of the hewing process. I started to hear His voice far more. I really needed to hear what He was saying. I needed to have truth to hold on to. I needed His encouragement and promises to cope with the relentless health setbacks and challenges of continuously feeling ill. I started to hear from God more than ever before. I look at my notebooks of where I record what He has said, and the level of input went up a significant degree after getting ill. I craved it and He knew I needed it. Very often it would come through other people having pictures or words from God, but I grew in receiving them myself. Not an audible voice, but when praying, I would be seeing images in my mind's eye, or get a phrase that would turn out to be absolutely relevant to whoever I was praying for. Some verses from the Bible would seem highlighted and be so pertinent. I would find God speaking through other things too; again as if what I was seeing was highlighted and with a sense of resonance in my spirit. I would find it would then be confirmed in other ways. There was a growing sense of discernment in my spirit of knowing when what I was sensing was from God and when it was just from me, and I learnt from the mistakes.

Another significant time stands out for me. I had had a big relapse in my recovery and was pretty weak. I had a growing sense that I should visit my friend in Canada, who lived out in the countryside, for my recuperation. It was a challenge as I wasn't strong enough to lift even hand luggage, but I knew it was of God to go. I also felt I was meant to go from there and visit a dear older lady in California, one of those saints who glow with God's Spirit. She had stayed at my parents' house for a while when I had been living there for six months, when I was too ill to live in my own home. This whole trip required a lot of faith, but I was up for it and I knew if it was of God, I would be OK.

Then commenced a crazy sequence of events with the flights. All my flights were delayed so much that I missed my connections. I arrived in Canada on a later flight than planned, which meant my friend had time to meet me in the arrivals hall. She had originally asked me to go across the car parks to meet her there, as she wouldn't have time to get to the arrivals hall. I suppose I had been hopeful that I would be able to manage that walk with my suitcase, but I wasn't being realistic and it was a definite concern. With missing my connection and arriving on a different flight, God overruled and showed His love in a very practical way.

I was more concerned about the trip to California as I couldn't see how either I or the elderly friend I was visiting would manage to lift my suitcase into her car. With that trip, they spilt diesel over the tarmac when refuelling the plane, so the flight had to wait an hour for it to be cleaned up. I consequently missed my connecting flight. On arrival I found my suitcase had been put on a different flight to me, so they delivered it to the door instead! These small incidents carry so much of God's love and care and faithfulness. Even though there were other practical solutions to my suitcase issues, God graciously showed that He cared. These moments, although seemingly trivial, stay with you for life and so prove that when you are weak, He is strong.[100]

My five weeks in Canada were so helpful for my health. It was an enormous gift to be able to rest so well and not use up the small amount of energy I had on the usual household chores. I could completely relax, leaving everything else behind in the UK. Spending a lot of time outdoors and gradually building up exercise each day, I grew stronger. I completely unwound, deeply relaxed and slept incredibly well.

A significant moment for me happened in California. We had a prayer time together that brought me peace. I had been struggling with a huge concern of: 'Was I missing something?' I was worried that there might be something I had missed praying about. Was there a spiritual root or foothold of the adversary that needed to be broken off? Was I unnecessarily suffering? During the prayer time I had an incredibly clear picture from God in my mind's eye that effectively was saying

---

100.   2 Corinthians 12:9-10.

that this was a purifying process, like that used for gold. I wouldn't be able to move on from it until it had done its work. The person who emerged from it would be changed. I saw a person much more full of light, with far less of the distinguishing features of me visible, but rather, much more of Jesus radiating out from me. Instead of disappointment that this was clearly going to continue for a while, I felt a deep peace and sense of grace to carry on walking through it. I felt I had received what I was looking for and I could go home now. I did have another week back in Canada and then soon after arriving back in England I managed a 1,000ft climb in Scotland. The change in six weeks had been phenomenal.

Sadly, that level of health didn't last and I had many setbacks going forward, but I never went back to the level of weakness before the trip to Canada.

Rising up out of the flames, transformed.

Without being ill and God leading me, I would never have had the courage to become self-employed and work part-time, but how wonderful that has been, especially as He has provided the work over and over again. Self-employment really suits me and it is so good to have space for other things. He knew the desires of my heart and how to get me there.

Over the years, I have been to several Christian places and people who carry a healing gift from God. It has been significant, seeing what has occurred each time. At the first healing prayer session I went to, they hardly prayed about the illness at all. When they asked God how to pray for me, He showed them a red-brick building. I immediately knew that it was my secondary school. A lot of deep pain from that time was released during the prayer session. God was showing me that His top priority was healing the whole me, not just the illness.

Secondary school had been a difficult time for me, as I know it can be for many. I found myself in a very difficult situation throughout the first term. This greatly knocked my confidence and caused deep wounds. I had further knocks in later years in school and found myself withdrawing into myself and putting up walls of protection. After leaving school, life was considerably easier and I flourished. However, at times, I would momentarily find myself feeling like thirteen-year-old me and would feel irrationally hyper-self-conscious and ill at ease. There had been layers of healing, but more was needed.

My search for healing and for how to fix my situation was leading me to more healing of the whole me. How often do we just plough on in our lives until something brings us up short? The illness pushed me to look deeper, to go on a thorough search for why I was ill; for any other root causes of the illness.

I had caught debilitating Lyme disease from a tick bite; it had made me very ill, in addition to chronic fatigue syndrome. This had taken a huge toll on my physical well-being. Yet I knew there had to be more going on; otherwise, why was I not healing quicker? Others who had the same medical treatment as I did were recovering far more quickly.

My search led to discovering many aspects of healing. Healing is rarely just physical. I began to see more about myself, and God started bringing things to the surface to deal with. I was living too much in my mind and not listening enough to the true me. I saw how much I avoided conflict and the difficult conversations. I saw key situations where I had not been honest with myself to avoid hurting others, and paid a big price in my own stress levels, which then caused significant health relapses.

God was taking me on a journey to heal up what had been sown into my soul during the school experiences. Here was the 'slave' mindset being exposed, being brought to the surface. It was time for it to be properly healed. A friend had had a picture from God for me of Gulliver on the ground, tied up with all the small ropes that were holding him down. They weren't huge ropes, but lots of small ones. (Gulliver, in the story *Gulliver's Travels*,[101] gets shipwrecked onto an island of tiny people. He awakes to find they have tied him up with lots of small ropes.) There wasn't one cause of the illness, or delay in recovery; there wasn't one easy fix, but there were a lot of small roots and areas to look into.

This can be true for so many people. We don't see ourselves as particularly messed up. We see inner healing and counselling as for other people, those with obvious big issues. There is a verse

---

101.   Jonathan Swift, *Gulliver's Travels* (Ware: Wordsworth Editions, 1992).

that says 'You desire truth in the innermost being'.[102] These little ropes, even the small areas of our thinking that aren't based on truth, these really matter to Him. They hold us back, they trip us up, they affect our well-being, our relationships, our ability to truly know how much God loves us, and they limit how God can use us.

I went back to those school memories with Jesus and saw Him with me there in each memory. In the first classroom, I saw Him holding a fragile bird in His hand which He then launched into the air to fly. He was saying those experiences launched me. They had shown me a need for God on a totally new level, which had been the beginning of a journey in God that has been the most powerful, wonderful thing in my life. He showed me truth about the situation and how it had falsely affected my view of myself. I had various people to forgive. I had a false identity to shed and lies I was believing about myself to bin. There was some very deep pain to let out and to hand over to Jesus. It was incredibly releasing and freeing to see it from God's perspective, from a place of truth. So I revisited every painful school memory with Jesus and saw Him in each, either lifting me up, protecting me, or speaking to me. It was as if He rewrote the memories. The pain has gone from them and I see them in the light of His truth, rather than from my teenage interpretations of the events.

I have gone back to defining moments in my life that were damaging, and found God healing and redeeming them. They have now transitioned to moments of deep insight into myself, times of growth and doorways into the Father's heart. He has exposed the things that took root in those moments and freed me from them.

---

102. Psalm 51:6, NASB.

Held in His hands and launched to fly.

We so often interpret painful situations incorrectly when we are young, and also even when we are older. I have seen this repeatedly in facilitating inner healing prayer. From these sessions, I would also say that about 90 per cent of people that come believe core lies about themselves, along the lines of not being good enough, or not really believing God loves them. They struggle to receive the truth that God's unconditional love is for them, by His grace, unmerited, because He simply loves them.

It is so clear to see now that God used the school experiences as a training ground to grow a calling in me to get alongside the wounded and broken. The adversary may have intended to wound me, tie me up, knock my confidence and instil fears into me, but God has cleansed, healed and overturned all of that. God has turned it round for good purpose.[103]

---

103. Romans 8:28.

Walking through the illness then added a further depth to that equipping.

Another Christian healing event stands out for me. I went to a healing conference in Bristol and went forward during an opportunity to receive prayer for healing. I felt the presence of God a little and it was nice but nothing significant happened. Later on, three people spoke of God healing them from chronic fatigue syndrome. God was clearly saying He could do that . . . but it was not yet my time, or there were more things to deal with first. However, the next day they had a time for prayer for people leading churches or ministries of any sort to receive impartation of more of God's power, especially in the area of healing. As I had no 'official' capacity, I didn't go forward for prayer. But then moments later, I felt the presence and power of God come on me extremely strongly, probably more than I had ever felt before, and it lasted a long while. During that experience, I asked God what was going on, what this was about. I immediately saw a mini vision of myself in a scenario that I have a huge heart for. I came away from the conference with a renewed passion for what I believe God was (and is) calling me to. I was hearing again the very clear message that me getting well right now was not the most important thing. There was something much bigger going on. This journey was not just about me, by any means. It was very much about equipping me for other people's healing too.

So, moving on to another healing prayer experience (in the United States) . . . this time it was about finishing the journey. During the prayer time, I very clearly saw an image in my mind's eye of being at the top of a mountain and planting a flag. I felt the presence and power of God on me very strongly and the picture impacted me profoundly. I had had many people over the previous few years see pictures, when praying for me, of me being close to the top of a mountain, but unable to get up the last sheer rock face. In my own ability, it was not possible to make that last climb. In this new picture, I was at the top. The summit was in cloud and I couldn't see much of the view. I was wearing a mountaineering coat, thick with snow from battering snowstorms. I was also wearing a rucksack of survival equipment that I no longer needed. I had the sense that it would be a while before I could appreciate that I had arrived at the top. I needed to recover from the exhaustion and toll of the climb and the clouds needed to go. I also needed to take off the rucksack of survival equipment.

After the appointment, I went to an Art Sozo[104] session (to meet with God's truth and healing through painting, using just sponges and paint). I had such a clear sense as I went with the flow of the Holy Spirit, that there was celebration in heaven that day. I saw a waterfall of joy and praise in the heavens, because I had made it to the top. The hosts of heaven were rooting for me, they were celebrating . . . and that undid me. To feel that I hadn't been alone, that many in heaven were watching, cheering me on, probably praying and today celebrating over me, was very humbling and very moving.

Later that day I picked up my book of devotional readings and the day's reading was about Zechariah (John the Baptist's father, in the New Testament). It was relating the time when an angel appeared to him to tell him his (presumably enduring) prayer for a child had been answered.[105] For him it would be a few months later before he would see the arrival of the baby. Again, this was the same message as arriving at the top of the mountain;

104.   www.artsozo.com (accessed 13.8.21).
105.   Luke 1:13.

even if it didn't feel like it yet, even if I couldn't fully see and appreciate it, the prayer had been answered.

I went to the Sunday evening service and partway through, someone stood up and said God had just shown them a scene of a rugby match. The player with the ball had a clear run to the goal line. He hadn't yet got there, but the stadium was on its feet in jubilation, as there was no question that he would make it. He was so nearly there, with an unhindered run. There was a theme to what I was hearing!

That evening, I went to my room with the big question of: 'Is this all real? Is this You, God, or is this a load of coincidences and my imagination?' The moment I sat on my bed, the presence of God came strongly into the room and stayed very tangibly, very thick, until the moment I finished writing it all up, and then it immediately lifted. It was the message: 'Yes, it is from Me. Trust Me.'

A few days later, I thoroughly enjoyed a slow, four-hour walk in Yosemite National Park, by far the longest and steepest walk I had done in years. We went via the top of one of the waterfalls, and very significantly, I was not ill the next day or low on energy. The waterfall was pure power and absolutely stunning. We were told the waterfalls were the best they had been in a decade. A long drought had ended and there had been far more snow than usual that winter. We had come at the time of the winter snow melt. This resonated powerfully with an image I had had a few days earlier of seeing the tears shed through the illness being transformed into a beautiful waterfall of power.

The image of the rucksack of survival equipment stayed with me, but I wasn't clear what it meant. What was it and how could I take it off? A while later I was reading a book on healing from trauma,[106] to have more understanding for facilitating inner healing prayer. The book was talking about how we usually see trauma as the big events such as war, car accidents, or abuse – but we can miss seeing smaller issues as trauma. Challenging events when we were young or at times of low emotional resources can cause trauma. They may be events that we would not now see as that traumatic, but for us then, they were. Illness can also cause trauma. Trauma can remain in our physical body, causing us to not feel fully safe, maybe at a subconscious level. This can trigger the body to react overprotectively, as a hyper-vigilant survival response.

Tears transformed to power.

106. Peter Levine, *Healing Trauma* (Boulder, CO: Sounds True, 2008).

It then dawned on me, the rucksack of survival equipment at least partly represented my body's survival response to trauma. It also confirmed a picture God had given me of my soul and spirit being in a good place, in the light, but my body in fear. I then had some inner healing prayer ministry. With Jesus I revisited times of trauma, I felt my body calming down and coming into a much deeper sense of rest and being grounded. I spent more time in meditative prayer, just repeating a phrase such as 'Jesus is Lord' for a while. This would bring me to a stilled and peaceful place, where it was as if my whole being was praying. Then I would soak in the peace of God. I also repeatedly spoke to the fear in my body and told it to go, in Jesus' name (with His authority). This, along with some grounding exercises, all helped to calm down the 'tired but wired' trauma response. I started sleeping better and feeling better.

God was leading me into other aspects of healing: understanding more about trauma, and its effect on the body. Many other illnesses, physical pain and mental health conditions can have their roots in emotional stress and trauma. Whilst facilitating inner healing sessions, I have seen over and over again God bringing beautiful healing to past trauma. When the trauma is healed, He then helps coping mechanisms relax, 'walls' come down, and mindsets, anxiety and other conditions are restored to wholeness.

Another significant moment revealed some of the 'plunder' and the equipping for Promised Land living. At one Sunday service at a church I was visiting, a person next to me asked me to pray for healing for cancer. Instantly I saw a huge, translucent cockroach-like creature covering their back. When I say I saw it, it was like an inner sight superimposed on what I was seeing in reality. I also saw a translucent spear that I knew was filled with the blood of Jesus. So in my mind's eye I took hold of the spear and speared the creature as I prayed, commanding the cancer to leave in Jesus' name. I repeated this five times and suddenly, on the fifth time, I saw the creature fall off and disappear. At precisely the same moment, with split second timing, the person doubled up forwards at 90 degrees, exactly the motion you would expect if you were unexpectedly released from a huge weight on your back. I believe they were healed. Both they and I were visitors to the church, so I had no way of finding out. But I have prayed for various people for physical healing over the years and each time when there was complete miraculous healing, I just knew deep within me they would be healed, and they were. It was as if I received a gift of faith each time. I had the same sense with this person.

This felt like stepping into more of the Promised Land living; walking in more of the authority Jesus gives us. It was an example of finding that there has been an *equipping*; to be able to discern more of what is really going on and of how to act and pray more powerfully.

Through this journey, there has been an unfolding understanding of how God heals the whole person. We often need emotional, psychological and spiritual healing, as well as maybe physical healing; which are often all interconnected. It has not only been a journey of finding that for myself, but of being equipped to walk alongside others to help them find it too.

The journey up the mountain has essentially been about the inner journey through a wilderness season and coming into a Promised Land. Navigating ill health and loss has been a part; but it's been far more than that, and it's a journey that continues.

There has been a sense that a lot of this journey has been about 'coming home'. A process in coming home to myself rooted in God; of finding the whole me, the full me, and being connected and at rest in who I am. It is also about coming to a deeper place of rest or being at home in God. When you know you are truly, truly loved by our heavenly Father, it brings you to a place of rest.

*The roots of our lives cleansed, healed
and at home in the Living Water.*

To Conclude

Whether God chooses to heal instantly, or over a period of time, or in the next life, is a mystery. A week after a close friend was diagnosed with cancer, not knowing her diagnosis, someone else – also recently diagnosed with cancer – asked my friend to pray for them . . . and that person was completely healed there and then. My friend had considerable amounts of prayer for her cancer over the next year . . . and she ended up in the better place, in heaven. At university, I prayed for a friend who had been in bed with glandular fever for a lot of the term, and she was completely healed; a dramatic difference the next day. This was the same illness that initiated chronic fatigue syndrome for me. So I've never had any doubt that God could have healed me rapidly at any point. He chose another outcome; a deeper healing, a greater equipping and much learning and transformation along the way.

Sometimes when our prayers seem to go unanswered, God is actually answering our deepest prayers and longings. When I was young, I prayed many, many times that my life would count, that it would be worth living, that there would be value in it. I couldn't bear the thought of getting to the end of my one and only life and finding it hadn't really been of value. God has used the things of life that I have had to walk through to change me, equip me and take me in the direction of answering that deepest longing. Along this journey, I have found an amazing, loving heavenly Father who has carried me and consistently provided for me. I have had to learn to lean on God and follow the promptings of the Holy Spirit in a very practical way (even in the seemingly small details of my life). This has been necessary, in order to arise from weakness and suffering and amazingly find joy in the midst of it all. I know it has been worth it.

With raku firing of pottery, the pot is fired in a fire pit with a variety of leaves, metals and other objects rubbing up against it. All of these impart colourful hues from their minerals into the clay. Every pot emerges from the fire unique and unreproducible. The fire leaves its mark by etching beautiful tones into the fabric of the clay. And the clay itself is transformed into a strong ceramic that can withstand incredible temperatures. It emerges with strength, dignity and beauty. The shades of mineral deposits will mark it forever, not as scorch marks, but as brushstrokes of beauty.

What we have gone through is part of who we are, and it will always be there. However, when it is remoulded and healed in the loving hands of our God, when it has been cleansed and purified with His grace and forgiveness, when the impurities have risen to the surface and gone, then our sufferings will have been transformed into beauty and strength.

The fire has been developing the beauties of a deep compassion, a gracious humility and a delicate tread to walk alongside the wounded without judgement. God has been beautifying us with the radiance of knowing we are His beloved. We have been discovering the treasured gold that comes from walking through the fire and finding that He was indeed faithful.

What we have gone through,
now healed and redeemed,
shines through as beauty.

For this light momentary affliction is preparing for us
an eternal weight of glory beyond all comparison

2 Corinthians 4:17

'This light momentary affliction is preparing for us an eternal weight of glory'.[107] This is a hard verse to read when the fire is raging. The lick and heat of the flames feel far from 'light' or 'momentary'. Perhaps we can't see the gold in us yet and maybe

---

107.   2 Corinthians 4:17, ESV.

we are not meant to. Yet we do get glimpses of how we have changed and how we are no longer the person we used to be. Dying to ourselves being in control or being number one, and letting God sit on the throne of our lives produces eternal gold. This opens the way for Him to work and radiate His life out to a broken and desperate world.

So, there have been many facets to what God has been doing through the illness. There has been a shedding of old thought patterns, a healing of the inner me, and a new sense of my identity in God. There has also been an equipping for living out God's purposes and a new authority in prayer. There is a now a walking into a Promised Land. There are still giants to face, but the desert environment has gone and I have been changed. I am now finding the privilege and joy of seeing strongholds coming down in other people's lives, truth coming into their thinking and seeing them rise up in their true identity in God, changed and set free.

I haven't wanted to write about how long or tough the illness has been, as all our journeys are different and my journey won't be yours. I am in no way suggesting that we need to go through rough times to grow close to God. Let's always pursue the riches of His love and the fullness of His Spirit within us.

What I hope has come through these pages is that though we may not understand why difficult things happen to us, God can be found right at the centre of adversity. He can turn it around for good. He can use it to change us, heal us, equip us and bring us so much closer to Him. His top priority is rarely to just fix our immediate issues and let us carry on just the same as we were. His greater purpose is to heal their root causes. He wants to heal the whole person. He wants to redeem the knocks that come against us from living in this imperfect world. He wants to heal us of the sufferings we brought upon ourselves from our own mistakes. He wants to set us free from the chains and afflictions of the adversary. What was meant for evil, God wants to turn around for good.[108]

We live in a broken world. Humankind's selfish, corrupt, wrongful ways have brought much suffering and have exacerbated poverty and disease, for which God is absolutely not to blame. He has given us free will, and we have made a mess of this world. Cultures have idolised things that are superficial and shallow and in direct contradiction to God's ways. People treat each other out of their own pain and brokenness causing immense damage, and this perpetuates down the generations. Yet so often we blame God for the famine, the diseases and sufferings humankind has brought upon itself.

However, in our lives, God can powerfully bring good out of bad and He wants to redeem every experience of pain and turn it into a gateway for transformation. So, if we are finding that life is tough, or things have been stripped away, or we just don't feel like we are having any fruitfulness in our lives, or we may be wondering, 'What is the point?', it could well be that God has drawn us aside into the wilderness to do a deeper work. Maybe it is time for a more fundamental healing, a greater transformation and an equipping to lead a powerful and fruitful life. Let's not get disillusioned, but instead see the fork in the road; the choice to seek God's way forward. The journey that goes deep into God's heart and into our own souls; that changes us and leads us out as victors.

---

108. Genesis 50:20.

Rising up in a struggling world.

Romans 8:19 says that 'creation waits in eager expectation for the children of God to be revealed'. It is saying the world is struggling; the world is desperate for God's people to rise up transformed and carrying His likeness and His power. We are God's children and He wants us to be healed up and radiating the nature of the true identity of His family; becoming more like Jesus.

The fires that we may go through are part of the transformation process that is so necessary, not only for our own well-being, but also for the world at large. God is calling us to be overcomers; to be people who, with God's help, win the battles; people not defeated by the plans of the adversary, but instead who turn them round for victory and plunder.

The adversary came to 'steal . . . kill and destroy', but Jesus came that we might have life 'to the full'.[109] Let's persevere, with God, to destroy the power of the adversary in our lives and take hold of everything that God has for us. Let's surrender into His arms of love, receive a complete healing and be powerfully equipped by His Spirit to be those people that creation is longing for.

It is true there is a cost in following Jesus; it is true the adversary will try many ways to discourage us, distract us, or derail us. Yet if we can change our *top* priority from trying to fix our immediate problems and instead see that God is calling us to something so much higher, so much deeper, so much richer, so desperately needed by this broken world, then the costs don't matter so much, the bruises don't last so long. He carries us through the suffering, the joys increase and we become changed people. We connect to an Almighty source of healing power and love and everything this world needs. When we find what we were

---

109. John 10:10.

made for, when we live for something so much higher, for God's purposes for our lives, we arise and we ascend. When we yield to the deepest love that heals our souls, when we shut all the doors to the adversary, when we connect to the almighty source of grace, love and sustaining power, then we truly rise up, and *'in all ... things we are more than conquerors'*.[110]

No, in all these things we are more than conquerors through him who loved us. For I am convinced that neither death nor life, nor angels nor demons, neither the present nor the future, nor any powers, neither height nor depth, nor anything else in all creation, will be able to separate us from the love of God that is in Christ Jesus our Lord.

Romans 8:37-39

---

110. Romans 8:37, emphasis mine.

Appendix 1

Sample Prayers

Prayer to commit your life to God

Father God, I know that I have lived life my own way and with my own wisdom, not in the way You intended for me to live. I am sorry for everything I have done wrong in thought or action. I am sorry I have lived my life without You at the centre. I am truly sorry, and now I want to turn away from this way of living. Please forgive me, help me and wash me clean. I believe that Your Son, Jesus Christ, died for me, was resurrected from the dead, is alive and hears my prayer. I invite Jesus to become the Lord of my life, to rule and reign in my heart from this day forward. Please send Your Holy Spirit to live in me and give me Your strength and love and peace. Help me to follow Your ways and live for You now. In Jesus' name I pray, Amen.

Prayer to receive forgiveness

Father God please forgive me for . . . I'm sorry for every aspect of what I have done wrong in my thoughts, attitudes and actions. I'm sorry for allowing this in my life. I now want to turn away from these behaviours/attitudes/thoughts and I ask You to set me free from the power they have had in my life. I ask You to forgive me and wash me clean. On the basis of Your forgiveness I choose to forgive myself. I choose to let go of self-condemnation and guilt and shame, and I give these to You and ask You to release me from them. I thank You that Jesus took what I deserved on Himself on the cross, that I might be forgiven and set free.

Prayer to forgive others

I choose to forgive ……………… for ……………… and the resulting consequences in my life. I choose to fully forgive them for the wounds and hurts they have caused me. I choose to hand over this person/situation/event to You and let go of my anger and unforgiveness.

Lord, I ask You to forgive me for any wrong reactions to the consequences in my life (fear, revenge, self-rejection, etc.) and for having any wrong attitudes (carrying an offence; unforgiveness; resentment; bitterness; retaliation; deception, etc.). I release them from my judgement and I hand them over to you. And in so doing I want to claim the same freedom for myself. I surrender the right to anything I feel they still owe me in the way of an apology or explanation. Jesus, I ask You to bless them.

You may need to choose to forgive many times until you know you have fully forgiven and let go.

Prayer to be set free

It is best to pray this prayer with another believer who already knows freedom in this area. Come to this time with an attitude of 'please show me any blind spot and absolutely anything that may be wrong'. Give plenty of space for God to bring things to mind. It is important to remove all 'rights' for the adversary to afflict you.

Lord, please show me any attitude, activity, or behaviour I have participated in that has come from or is agreeing with the dark realm, or has opened a door to the dark realm, or is keeping me from inner freedom. Please show me anything I need to stop doing, or any attitude that needs to change.

I choose to fully turn away from . . . and ask for Your forgiveness and Your help to change.

I turn away from any involvement in New Age, witchcraft, or occult activities. I reject the beliefs and I renounce and break all allegiance, oaths and covenants with Freemasonry, witchcraft, or the occult that I have made knowingly or unknowingly, or my ancestors or any of my partners or their ancestors have made. I forgive them for all their wrongdoing, wrong attitudes, for any way they opened a door to the dark realm and for any way this has affected me. Is there anyone I specifically need to forgive? . . . I choose to forgive . . .

I reject any false belief that these activities are OK or harmless. I ask You to forgive me for any way I have partnered with this realm in attitude, belief or action. I ask You, Jesus, that you revoke all oaths and cancel any resultant repercussions over my life [or my children][111] and set me free. I ask that You completely break off the hold of any power from Freemasonry, witchcraft, or the occult over my life [and my children][112] and set me free from any consequences in my life or my descendants' lives. I put the cross between myself and my ancestors.

I ask all this through the name and authority of Jesus Christ. Please wash me clean and fill me afresh with Your Holy Spirit. Replace every power that has had a hold on me with Your lordship and Your freedom. I thank You for Your forgiveness and Your power to set me free.

You may need to get further help and do more in-depth prayer in any areas mentioned above that you have been involved in directly or indirectly.

---

111. If appropriate.
112. If appropriate.

Appendix 2

Pause and Encounter

The *Pause and encounter* questions have been influenced by my training in (now called) Transform Prayer Ministry, Bethel Sozo and Christian counselling, but go wider and have come from much inner healing prayer ministry experience.

If this book has brought issues to the surface, or you have struggled with the *Pause and encounter* sections, you may find it helpful to pray through them again with someone else who easily hears from the Holy Spirit. It is often considerably easier to hear from God when praying with someone else. As Jesus said, 'where two or three are gathered together in my name, there am I in the midst of them.'[113]

You may also find the following inner healing prayer ministries helpful. As with everything, it is best to pray for God to show the way forward with this. What is helpful for one person may not be for another.

---

113. Matthew 18:20, ASV.

Bethel Sozo
www.bethelsozo.org.uk,
www.bethel.com/ministries/bethel-sozo-international

Transform Prayer Ministry
www.transformationprayer.org

Jesus Ministry
www.jesusministry.life

Restoring the Foundations
www.restoringthefoundations.uk

I am in no way endorsing every practitioner, or any mistakes or inexperience that may have happened under these umbrellas; however, Holy Spirit-led prayer ministry is a powerful and wonderful thing. I also do not necessarily endorse the way these ministries may evolve in the future. I never recommend stopping any medication against the advice of the medical profession.

Acknowledgements

I would like to give heartfelt thanks to the many people, my family and friends, who have helped and supported me in the writing of this book. I would particularly like to give thanks to my parents for many hours of help with editing and proof reading; to Grazyna, for editing the initial draft; to Sandy, Suzanne and Judy, for so much support with this book; and to my brother, and so many other friends who have reviewed manuscripts, or prayed and encouraged me through this time, and indeed through the many years of illness. I owe a huge debt of gratitude to you all.